Christie Bo

Chris Fraser, 1994

Copyright

Fraser & Son

Acknowledgements

The rare photographs of the early MacBrayne's steamers are included thanks to the generosity of the late Graham Langmuir. All are from his extensive, and probably unique, private collection now held at Glasgow's Mitchell Library. Others were generously provided by Ian McCrorie who has collected his own private archive of MacBrayne's memorabilia, and with the co-operation of Cal Mac.

The photographs of in-service MacBrayne's buses were kindly provided by John Sinclair, from his extensive archive. His book Highland Buses is available via Amazon. The admirable MacBrayne's Circle were also a great help.

I am grateful to the late Jim Aikman Smith, of the West Highland Steamer Club, for a few corrections to what he gently referred to as "misprints in the text" of the first edition.

Dedications

In 1994, my father dedicated the first edition to Absent Friends. Sadly with the passing of time, Christie himself and my mother Rena have joined them.

This revised edition of Christie's book would not have been possible without the encouragement (and typing skills) of my wife, Joanne.

Foreword

by Kit Fraser

1851

This was a landmark year for the United Kingdom. Londoners and visitors alike gasped at their first sight of the Great Exhibition, housed in the revolutionary Crystal Palace. A book, "A Study of Barnacles," was published by a little known naturalist. It was the first in a body of work that would lead the author, Charles Darwin, to establish the theory of evolution in "The Origin of Species".

The Highlands and Islands of Scotland had been blighted by the infamous potato famine for five long years, contributing to an exodus of approximately 90,000 people from the area - about a third of the population. Four years earlier, Queen Victoria reflected her growing affection for the area by sailing the Crinan Canal from Ardrishaig to Crinan, there joining the Royal Yacht.

In the shipping world, 1851 was the year G & J Burns decided to concentrate their business on Irish routes and their interest in Cunard, and handed over their West Highland Trade to their chief clerk, David Hutcheson. One of the conditions was that their nephew, David MacBrayne, would become one of the partners. In 1877, David Hutcheson retired, as did his brother Alexander two years later, leaving MacBrayne as the sole partner. The name of the company was changed to David MacBrayne.

A hundred years on from the launch of the company that would become MacBrayne's, their newly appointed manager in Inverness, Christie Fraser, would be presented with a son – me.

My early years were steeped in MacBrayne's, often visiting my father's office at Farraline Park, Inverness, the cramped bus station the company shared with Highland Omnibus. I remember the bustling nature of the terminus which resulted, on one occasion, in the near side front wing of a single decker intruding through the door of the MacBrayne's booking office as it negotiated its way out of a tight spot. The driver was left in no doubt that this was dangerous, careless and unacceptable, by the Agency Manager, Dad.

Most holidays were spent in Kyle of Lochalsh, staying with my grandparents, and Dad's eldest sister, Joey who cared for them. His brother, my Uncle Jack, drove the "Post" bus for MacBrayne's operation in Kyle, a Bedford Olaz. This was similar to the one on the cover, at, I think, Kyleakin, across the ferry from Kyle.

It was as a passenger in a similar Bedford, based in Inverness, that I had a close inspection of the bus's pedals. Dad had some business to do in Foyers, on Loch Ness side, and took me along for the ride. We sat behind the driver, in his open position, as the bus made its way along the single track road. Suddenly, around a blind corner, emerged a car, requiring a sudden, if not emergency, stop ! Whether I went over the driver's shoulder, or merely was lifted out of my seat and fell between him and the window, I don't know.....but I ended up having a close examination of the brake, clutch and accelerator pedals at his feet. I also don't know who was more shocked and apologetic – me, the driver or Dad. Happily, I escaped with a minor graze and, as Para Handy might have said, luckily did the bus no damage.

I don't think it's solely due to my formative years growing up with MacBrayne's buses, but I have a great affection for the iconic colour scheme applied to them. The piller box red bodywork, with black wheel arches, cream framed windows and, what an enthusiast tells me is, leaf green roof. Add the silhouettes of a sword wielding Highlander and lion rampant, and you have something that will, for me, forever be an intrinsic part of a Highlands' and Islands' landscape, now sadly gone. I have a model of just such a Bedford in my study to this day. I am not alone. The MacBrayne's Circle of enthusiasts, who have preserved and restored a small fleet of these vehicles, proves my point and I have given over a small post script to their admirable efforts.

Visits to Kyle from Inverness were via a straightforward railway journey. After Dad was re-located and, it appears, promoted to Fort William, however, our visits became more adventurous. We took the West Highland line to Mallaig from where we took the service steamer up the

The Lochseaforth

coast to Kyle. That was how I encountered the Lochnevis, I think the Lochmor, and the "big" boat, the Lochseaforth.As it turned out, I am no better a sailor than my father (see his own account later.) My memories of these trips are dominated by the, often, roughish crossing to Armadale and of the reek of fish and chips, from the restaurant, adding to my discomfort. My MacBrayne's memories of Fort William, still in the 50s, include sitting beside the folding door of the "modern" single decker, chatting to the friendly drivers, as I caught the service bus back from primary school in Banavie to our rented home, "The Bungalow", overlooking the former naval base at Corpach.

The King George V

Latterly, the family settled in a company house overlooking Loch Linnhe. I clearly remember the excitement of the spectacular King George V passing the house, on summer cruises from Oban, belching smoke from her twin stacks, and setting up an impressive bow wave which we greeted as it came ashore on the beach below our home.

I also remember watching Christie being presented to Her Majesty the Queen, on the MacBrayne's pier, during a Royal visit to Lochaber. A photograph of that event was displayed prominantly at home for many years. It seems, though, that the Royal Visit was an increasingly rare rewarding experience for Dad in his managerial role. Following one more disagreeable incident, detailed in his book, in 1961 he took his leave of the company he had served man and boy since 1928 and began a new life as Sub Postmaster in the sleepy, former railway junction, village of Aviemore.

In later years, after retiring from Aviemore Post Office, my mother, Rena, led a family campaign to get Dad to write down his fund of stories and memories. Over a period of time, this produced a series of hand written manuscripts, then transcribed via her typewriter. I managed to organise an early method of self publishing, which Dad financed, and his book saw daylight in 1994. With his health deteriorating, I was delighted to be able to finally hand him his life in print. Happily my efforts at marketing Christie Boy, by visiting or contacting book shops, plus the powerful force of word of mouth amongst Highlanders, saw the book sell out and more than cover Dad's outlay.

The family's connection with MacBrayne's was not to end there completely. Many years later, in my own career culminating as Political Correspondent for BBC Scotland, I was heavily involved in covering the battle to keep, what was by then, Caledonian MacBrayne, in public ownership. In what some critics might say was a rare piece of cleverly drafted legislation, the Scottish Government succeeded in retaining ownership, despite EU tendering rules.

Sadly my father didn't live to see that, passing on a year after Christie Boy was published and I'm not sure which side of the battle he would have been on. He would, however, have had a trade-mark chuckle when I was invited to talk to a Cal Mac staff conference, soon after I took the decision to stand down from Hollyrood and BBC Scotland in 2009. He would have had another when my friends and colleagues in Inverness presented me with a Cal Mac "hard hat".

There is one detail oddly omitted from Dad's autobiography. He makes only passing references to his skill as a footballer. In fact, during one of his games for the local club in Kyle, he was being scouted by Third Lanark, then a force in senior football. Unfortunately, he suffered a knee injury which saw him stretchered off the field. That was to be an injury that not only may have closed the door on a very different career but troubled him throughout his army service. It was his right knee. When I was 18, playing football for Stirling University, I too seriously injured my right knee. Many years later my elder son Alasdair injured his right knee. It has to be said, though, he had clearly inherited his grandfather's skills, like his brother Iain, rather than anything passed down from me. My father was left handed, like my grandfather. I am left handed too, as are my two sons.

I learned much later from a cousin that, in the extended family, Dad was known as the Storyteller. It is with sadness that I am aware many of Dad's stories didn't make it into his manuscript. Like his adventure returning from a ceilidh on Islay, by bike, at midnight, to meet the early morning ferry. Understandably, given the venue, a drop of two of “The Cratur” had been imbibed, which, predictably, had affected his balance. Before he'd gone far, a sudden imbalance put him in the ditch. Unharmed, he climbed out and set off again, only to, almost immediately, hurtle into the ditch again. When it happened a third time, he decided to stay where he was – upside down in a rhododendron bush. When he awoke, dawn was rising and he realised his problem – when first crashing into the ditch, he had twisted the handlebars off the straight. So, when remounting and steering down the road, the wheel, at an angle, took him straight back into the ditch !

The original edition of Christie Boy stemmed from the family's determination that his many written memories of a Highland way of life long gone and his entertaining tales of West Coast characters should not disappear with him. Nearly a quarter of a century later, I realise the case for publishing Christie Boy was just as strong today as in the 1990s. Having self published last year “The Triumph and Tragedy of the Bantams” - the story of the now overlooked Great War battalions of small men – I decided Dad's story should be made available to a new generation in the same way.

Contents

Part One

Tarmacadam had not yet come North

Chapter One

As daylight wanes on a late winter's afternoon and the fierce gusts of a North Westerly hurl hailstones against the windows, the bubbling firelight chases shadows across the ceiling and memory travels back over the years to another November evening in 1918. The setting is a small railway cottage some two miles from the village of Lairg, in Sutherland. A neighbour had just called in with news that Ross Culbuie had been reported missing, believed taken as a Prisoner of War. This was just the latest blow to an area where sadness was widespread, even affecting one young mind which somehow, in its naivety, connected the raging of the hailstorm with this whispered news.

I was then five years of age, having made my appearance at 6 o'clock of a winter's evening on 18th January, 1913. I'm told my entrance was anything but simple, aggravated by the late arrival of the medic. But thanks to the care of Mrs Mackay, Lower Torrible, an "Angel of Mercy" to all her neighbours in need, it was safely accomplished. Naturally it took me a year or two to come to terms with my surroundings but I soon took on. Although the Kaiser War had been in progress for two or three years before I got up to date, my world grew steadily as its contents were gradually revealed to me.
Our home was a semi-detached cottage with a large living room which included a bed in the corner and a small scullery just off. Two bedrooms upstairs completed the living accommodation. Water was obtained from an outdoor tap, shared with our neighbours. The "lavvy" was set in a birch wood at the end of the garden and occasioned many a cold trip for the poor unfortunate who had to travel "outwith normal hours."

Dad - Christopher – had been born in the Black Isle, across the Beauly Firth from Inverness, then moved to Ullapool when my grandfather got a job as a Telegraph Messenger on an estate there. In due course the family moved to Isle Martin, an island to the north of Ullapool, which they shared with another household. The family gradually increased and Dad went to work on a neighbouring estate. However as more sisters and brothers arrived, it was decided to move back to the mainland.

Dad moved with them and quickly found work at the Rose Street Foundry in Inverness which was at that time busy supplying the Highland Railway with all that was required for the extension North of the Highland capital. Before too long, though, he joined the Railway company itself as a Signalman. It was at Inverness Station, during an off-duty period, that Dad noticed a lady seeing a young man away on the train. As was his nature, he took a special interest in the young woman and, after the train had departed, greeted her, in the [passing, in Gaelic. Immediately there was a mutual interest, which was never to fail.
Mam – Margaret MacDonald – had been born and brought up on the Isle of Harris and left home to serve as a housekeeper in the Manse at Carrbridge. She very soon discovered that the requirements were not to her liking. Apparently the lady of the house had something of a weakness for a dram and had used Mam to obtain the whisky, behind her husband's back.

Seeking the counsel of the local Doctor, she was advised to change her work. On the Doctor's arrival home, he discussed the young woman's plight with his wife. It was decided to offer Mam a position in their household – a proposition she readily accepted. The result was a quick departure to Inverness and what Mam described as a wonderful feeling of freedom. She took up the post of housekeeper and one of her main jobs was to do all the home baking.

One morning the Doctor chose a sample of each batch and, unknown to Mam, entered them in the Highland Show, then a regular highlight of the Inverness year. There were seven items exhibited and each one fetched First Prize. In fact, if one other item had been exhibited, Mam would have been allowed to keep the Cup that was awarded. I can still taste her girdle scones.

It was not long before the Doctor and his wife discovered that Christopher was hanging about. Mam and Dad had become regular "dates" and on a Sunday spent much of the day walking miles to distant churches. It was obvious that, in time, there would be a wedding. When the date was decided, the Doctor was generous enough to undertake all the arrangements.

In due course the family began to appear, the first a girl, my eldest sister Joey, with additions arriving at regular intervals. Joey was brought up in the Gaelic language, which in "the English Town" of Inverness, was a mistake. When she started school she couldn't play with the other children and came home weeping. The result of this was that from that point the rest of the family spoke only English, leaving Man and Dad with a secret language which only Joey understood.

The family's first move was to Lairg, in Sutherland. By that time Joey had been joined by Murdo, Donald and Margaret (Mag). Typically, for that time, there had been two other boys who died in childbirth. I myself, Jackie, Isobel (Bella), Jessie and Annie (Nan) arrived in due course. This, then, made for a happy home and though many bad as well as good times were to be shared over the years, we remained a close-knit family all our days.

Obviously, there was no lack of company, and though we were the only young family in the immediate vicinity, we never suffered loneliness – and if ever anything untoward occurred in the area they didn't have far to look for the culprit.
Like others of the time, our life followed a general pattern in which large families were the norm and parents devoted their lives to the upbringing of their children. Although our house was small for the size of our family, and lacked all the facilities of a modern home, our parents successfully

fought to provide for all our needs, a near insurmountable task. Religious instruction heralded the beginning and the ending of each day and the fear of God lay deep in our beings when the ups and downs of daily life were accepted as just reward for previous behaviour. The churches condemned forms of work and recreation on the Sabbath, and few children appeared outdoors except to attend Church or Sabbath School.

At the appropriate times, in the morning and evening, the Fraser cavalcade could be observed making their way along Station Road, alongside the River Shin. The girls would be clad in frocks, collar, stockings and button-up boots, the boys in belted Norfolk jackets, celluloid collar, stockings and tackety boots, or sandshoes, depending on the season. Other than the footwear, everything had been fashioned by the loving hands of my mother and her constant companion, the Singer sewing machine.

Fortunately for us we learned, at an early age, that freedom could only be had on licence, and though many families would only appear in public at church service hours, our parents agreed to us being free to go for walks, as long as it was done quietly, in keeping with the Sabbath calm. On most occasions we succeeded in behaving well, or at least well enough to to escape discovery, But, inevitably, at times the standards dropped, particularly when visiting the railway station, which was always closed on Sundays.

As trains only broke the Sabbath in emergencies, it could be assumed that clattering of rolling stock meant that "Christie's Boys" were, once again involved with the surface man's bogey and were pushing around on the main line. The noise shattering the peace and quiet of the Sabbath. Dad would lose no time in positioning himself at the wicket gate through which we had to leave the yard. Equipped with his silver mounted walking stick, he meticulously applied it to our posteriors as we dashed through and escaping by another route only delayed the stroke until home.

Mam was never free from her household chores, and considered dressmaking and knitting light relief from drudgery while resting her feet. She regularly produced stockings and jerseys to protect us from the cold, cold winters of Sutherland. Her garments were much admired by the neighbours. Her prowess at tailoring short trousers was also remarkable, with the unfortunate exception that she never quite mastered the fitting of button flies, settling instead for a little slit which made for easy access.... but sometimes too easy escape.

The nearest shops were some two miles distant from the station and the Butcher's and Baker's vans called once a week. Most of our bread, however, was baked at home with ample supplies of griddle and oven scones, oatcakes and pancakes to fill the nooks and crannies of growing bodies.

Cakes were a luxury seldom seen, but in our large family the birthday “clootie dumpling” frequently made a welcome addition to our daily school “piece”. Milk and butter were obtained from Hector Mackay's croft at Gruids, while potatoes came from our own garden, along with those earned by the older children at the “tattie lifting” on neighbouring crofts and pitted by Dad to see us through the winter. Rabbit formed part of our staple diet, along with the odd piece of venison and, of course, trout, cold haddock, herring and cod roe, delivered by Esther, from Golspie, who called once a week.

During the fruit season jam making came into its own and wherever wild fruit was to be found - raspberries, brambles, gooseberries, black and red currants and rhubarb - we all played our part in the picking. The usual target for our larder was 100lbs. and was nearly always achieved with some fruit gifted by those who had it to spare.

As the family grew in years and stature, footwear and suiting had to be purchased from city suppliers whose representatives travelled round the villages and crofts at the spring and Fall of the year. Hamilton Murray, Glasgow, were well known suppliers in those days and were astute enough to employ a rep with local family connections. Mr. Murray was very popular in the area and generally succeeded in his quest for orders. If he was lucky he also got paid the outstanding balance from the previous year's order.

Mail order was then commonplace and our family orders also included bolls of flour and oatmeal, tea and sugar,cocoa, golden syrup and treacle and unfortunately, large jars of cod liver oil and malt extract. This last concoction arrived in a jar displaying a fisherman clad in oilskins and knee boots, with a large fish slung over his shoulder, and was believed to ward off winter chills.   It was generally dispensed at bedtime, with Dad moving round his flock armed with a big spoon. When news reached us that Hamilton Murray's order was at the station the excitement was intense and there were plenty of willing hands available to help with the take-home.

At this time in my life, despite the Country having been at war for some years, my whole world revolved around around the railway station. Already the engine drivers were known to us by their proper or “by-names” awarded by their workmates, or “characters” who circulated in profusion then. The Highland Railway's green engines were our mutual friends: the Lochs, Castles, Wee Bens , Big Bens, Barneys, and last but not least, Snaigo and Durn.

These early days presented a picture of uniformed men arriving and departing, impossible tales of German U-boats seen moving in the River possibly to discourage us (from going near there) and the strange “Americans” said to be near Bonar Bridge. Each night as we prepared for bed we sneaked a lookout of the front door to see the shafts of searchlights sweeping the night sky above Invergordon, on the look-out for Zepplins. As we listened to our older brothers repeating the news of those missing and killed, we cowered in our beds with minds full of imags and feelings known only to bairns of that age.

Lairg Station was then the railhead for North-West Sutherland in addition to the Lairg district, and I was introduce to the inner workings of the rail system at an early age. Arthur Chisholm, the booking clerk of the time became my guardian with whom I spent most of my waking hours. How he put up with it I will never know! I accompanied him out to the Catcher Point whenever the Jellico (troop train) was signalled. On hearing her approach from Invershin, the catcher arm was removed from its box, fitted into position, and I was bunged into the box in case I was carried away in the slipstream. I can still savour the feeling of sitting in the dark, shaking with the increasing vibration of the approaching train and then the shattering noise as it hurtled passed on its way to Scrabster.

The Catcher was an ingenious system introduced to exchange tablets when, through human error, the transfer failed,and the express,not permitted to proceed without a tablet,had to pull up and come back for it. This was not always as easy as it would seem. Sometimes the disc had disappeared into the trees, and it was common practice for everyone, including the passengers, to take part in the search. One one occasion, the tablet had got firmly wedged in the top branch of a tree, and was missing for three days. During that time all trains in that sector had to be preceded by a pilot engine to ensure the safety of the passengers.

On another occasion, after a heavy fall of snow, the platform staff took the easy way out by sweeping all the snow from the platform onto the track. This was, no doubt, in the hope that a thaw would do the rest before Monday when services were resumed. They had forgotten, however, that a special fish train from Wick was due to pass through in the early hours of Sunday morning. The result was that the engine's snowplough threw up huge lumps of snow, which had now hardened, leaving the station buildings with few windows intact.

Snowblocks were frequent in the Northern area, mostly in Caithness,

Forsinard, Scotcalder and Georgemas Junction. Once the Jellicoe was stuck at Forsinard for two weeks with snowdrifts like haystacks. With great excitement we watched two big engines fitted with the "big plough" which enveloped the engine from rail level to funnel, pass through Lairg on their way to successfully attack the block.

Mail and passenger services had extended onto Lochinvar, Scourie, Durness, Tongue and all points between, by road. Tarmacadam had not yet come north and passengers were few, so the limited accommodation provided by the Ford "Tin Lizzies" was generally taken up by the mails and odd bits of goods picked up at the station or originating from Lairg itself. These routes were difficult to maintain. In winter snows they were often closed for periods of several days and sometimes even weeks.

The principle commodity for export was rabbits and hampers of them arrived daily at the station for dispatch to the North of England, in particular to Leeds and Blackburn. It was one of those days that a large consignment of hampers had been weighed and loaded on to a three-wheeler trolley. It required moving across the yard to the platform for loading onto the next train. The approach to the platform, served by a narrow passage, was blocked by a carelessly parked "Tin Lizzie". The porter was being assisted by Mr. Budge, the Station Master, who nipped over and pushed the Ford out of the way.

Unfortunately the van had been left in gear and had jumped to life, setting off on a circuit of the square where it was frantically pursued, by the station master. No doubt, the perplexed man was familiar with the working of locomotives but he had no idea how to deal with a runaway van. Regardless, he flung himself onto the vehicle running-board, his hands grabbing at the levers inside the cab, inadvertently advancing the throttle, whereupon the van leapt forward with new found vigour and headed straight for the fence. It bounced back at the first attempt, but on the second effort the front wheels clambered up and over the top, the engine failed, and the vehicle slowly collapsed on to its side.

All this time, Mr. Budge was rubbing his elbow which had taken a nasty knock from a fence post and the staff were collecting to find out if he was unhurt. My brother Jack and I had witnessed the whole show and unknown to them all, were witnessing the swelling of a part of the inner tube which had broken free from the front tyre. We were now waiting with bated breath for the bang – which duly occurred. - and added an encore to the pantomime just completed.

There was always something happening around the station. One memorable incident comes to mind when an up and coming ornithologist had cadged a lift on a goods train. He and his two dogs were ensconced in the guards van at the rear of the train which had just left Lairg Station. They were heading north towards Rogart and had passed over the level crossing at the North Cabin. The engine driver was giving as much throttle as possible to negotiate the steep gradient when a coupling between two wagons gave way. Before the driver realised it, he was only pulling half of his train. The rear portion, including the guards van, had not only stopped but had already started moving back downhill. The guard applied his handbrake but soon realised it was no match for the weight and decided it was time to abandon ship.

It is not known why he was not joined by his fellow traveller and his "twa dugs" but in no time the runaway portion was in full flight. Dad was the signalman on duty who had so recently signalled the train through at the North Cabin. He had just re-opended the level crossing to road traffic and was in the act of leaving for the station. Taking a last look round, he spotted the approaching "part train." His quick response certainly saved the train, one man and his dog. He re-opened the gates, set the points and sprinted for all he was worth to the South Cabin to open the through passage for the train. He was in time to see the breakaway hurtle passed the cabin with a bewildered white face at the window of the van. The portion ran for several miles before losing way on another gradient, near Culrain. Fortunately, there was no damage and there was no other train in the vicinity. In later hears, the stowaway was to become a well-known ornithologist and judge of piping but history does not relate if he ever availed himself of another goods train journey.

It was about this time that the Armistice was celebrated – at long last. Though some of the family were victims of a measles epidemic and brother Donnie, who was very delirious, complained that "the Australians were in his hands", those of the family able to share in the celebrations hoisted a Union Jack over the coal shed. The relief and happiness of this time was shortlived.

With the outbreak of Spanish Flu which raged throughout the land, many whole families were struck down and this was the case in our home. The only medicine being whisky, it was carefully spooned out to each member of the family by Mam, who rose from her sick bed to minister. It was indeed a tragic period, never to be forgotten by the villagers, when many of those who ecsaped the call-up for the services became victims of the flu. I can still see a funeral cortege wending its way over the Ord of Gruids bearing three coffins – two black and one white – the two parent Sutherlands and their youngest child. The surviving children were adopted by relatives on the West coast.

Tragedy struck our own family, in the untimely death of our youngest sister, Anne Jane, who was just in her third year. She had contracted a very bad cold which quickly turned to pneumonia. Though the doctor did what he could, it was to no avail and Anne passed away after only a fortnight's illness. It was the first time the younger members of the family had faced this final reality, though Duncan and Alex too, had died in infancy some years before when the family were still living in Inverness. Deep sadness pervaded the home and Mam, who had nursed the little one, day and night, was heartbroken.

It was decided that Anne would be buried in the family lair in Tomnahurich Cemetery in Inverness. I remember every moment of that morning to this day. While it was yet dark, the small cortege proceeded to the station and joined the early train for Inverness. Only my elder brother Don and Dad travelled, being joined by uncles Duncan and Jimmy Barron at Dingwall and Muir-of- Ord.

On arrival at Inverness, several of Dad's workmates carried the coffin to the station entrance where John Fraser, the Undertaker, with his hearse and pair took charge.This picture was conveyed to us by Donnie on his return and his graphic description of the pair of "Greys" (apparently used when the remains were of a young person – at other times the "Blacks" were employed) and how they bowed their heads when the coffin was placed in the hearse, impressed and touched our young hearts. Inverness was still a rural town and it was the practice for all traffic to come to a stands still and give a clear passage to a funeral, while every man removed his had.

When we are young, however, sorrow, like a wet and stormy day is soon replaced by sunshine and life for us was a tremendous adventure. Summer arrived on the first fine warm day when tackety boots and thick stockings became uncomfortable and were discarded as soon as the school "scaled" and we were out of sight. Stuffing the stockings into the boots, we tied them together by the laces and slung them over our shoulders. Then we crept, gingerly, home over the smooth sheep-track which was part of the road in those days.

This was the start of the "barefoot season" (except for church, of course). Within days the soles of our feet were as tough as leather. Apart from the occasional stubbed toe, we stayed comfortably this way throughout the summer. Only the approach of autumn frosts plus, of course, the arrival of Hamilton Murray's latest order, ended this style for another year.

On one memorable occasion, I was to learn that there were certain areas where bare feed were a definite disadvantage. To wit, a newly mowed cornfield wearing a healthy stubble! I was helping a neighbour by taking her cattle out to grazing in the morning and fetching them home in the evening. The crofters of the time usually had one milker, a maturing heifer and a calf. This time “Rosie” supplied the milk, “Daisy” was the young heifer and the calf had not yet been christened.

On the way home, I noticed that Daisy was acting peculiar, occasionally jumping onto Rosie's back. I became very worried about it and reported the matter to Christina when we reached the byre. She accepted the report quietly and told me that, if that was the case, I would have to take Daisy to see Mr MacDonald, Balloan Farm, on Saturday morning.The day dawned bright and clear and |I found Daisy already wearing a headrope, prepared by Willie the Slater, brother of Christina. Barefooted, I set off for Balloan and the journey was unspectacular. I became aware then that another cattle beast was keeping step with us on the other side of the fence and seemed unusually interested in Daisy. With a steady gait we were there in no time and had to wait for Mr.MacDonald to finish breakfast. He took control, while I tried,very earnestly to explain to him the peculiar antics of Daisy – but he didn't appear to think it was anything very serious.

The opening of the gate and a flurry of activity left poor Daisy wondering what had hit her - and me, furious at such treatment of an animal. I accused Mr. McDonald of cruelty but he was quite unmoved and spoke to me quietly assuring me that Daisy would be fine now and I could take a shortcut through the cornfield and out through the gate to reach the main road.

I still had faith in him – after all he was a leading elder of the Church - but I felt it was a poor show. Within the next few minutes I was to learn the some more truths about the strange Facts of Life. Daisy began to kick up her heels and shake her head before breaking into a gallop. Now was the time when I could have done with my tackety boots. In no time, I was being dragged behind a berserk animal, and with bleeding feet, I had to let go and leave her to her own devices. The recently cut corn was stooked in groups of sheaves all over the field and by the time Daisy had finished tossing them up in the air they made a sorry sight. She did have enough sense, to wait at the gate for it to be opened and was then content to be led home by the head-rope.

We trotted happily home without further incident. I was content to be free of that daft animal and, no doubt, Daisy had her own happy thoughts! For the next week or two I gave a wide berth to Mr. Mac Donald, feeling really guilty about the way Daisy had treated his sheaves.
Pre-school education took the form of listening to the older children as they did their homework, with their books laid out on the living room table. School couldn't happen soon enough for us. My big day came along in due course and I joined the others on their way to Lairg Higher Grade School, situated in the village some two miles distant.

Apart from a few “Tin Lizzies” most transport was horse-drawn. This did offer us an advantage over many of the other scholars who hailed from outlying isolated areas, as there was always a chance of a lift. When these were on offer, we found ourselves with up to an hour to play before school went in. In addition to catering for pupils from the Lairg area, the school also took secondary pupils from North West Sutherland, who were able to qualify direct to University from there.

These pupils lived in boarding houses in the village, only getting home when the seasonal holidays came along. Many of the local scholars had long and exposed distances to cover, during the winter months, from Braemore, Achany, Terryside, Saval and other outlying townships. In recognition of this the School Board provided a “soup kitchen” where Mrs. Snoddy never failed to produce a warm bowl of soup or mug of cocoa for those in need. I'm sure she was ever-remembered with gratitude by the pupils of that time.

Hector MacKay, Sydney House, a native of the village who had recently returned form Australia and was farming Saval, will also be remembered as a benefactor to the school, particularly for providing sports gear. Sir

Edgar Horne, then the proprietor of Lairg Lodge supplied most, if not all, of the Class Prizes each year. If memory serves me right, the "General Knowledge" papers were set by him or with his assistance. My proud boast is that over the years I won three of those "General Knowledge Prizes."

To top that, I was capped to play for the First Eleven football team at the age of eleven - the school always produced a good side. The one I remember best being: Fergus Fortune, Tom Anderson (Clebrig), John and George Christie (Ault-na-Hara), Murdo Fraser, Murdo Boyce MacLeod, Andrew Dunbar Duncan (Tongue), Walter Davidson, Jock Rory and Eddy Simm.

The teaching staff were led by Mr. Henderson who carried his tawse in his pocket. A painful discovery I made after I had been caught on the window ledge during the temporary absence from the classroom of our teacher, Miss Munro. Mr. Henderson had walked into the room during a noisy session and had to pull me by the arm to come down before I discovered his presence. I still remember him removing the strap from his pocket and straightening it out across his knee before applying two-of-the-best......one to each hand. The retreat to my seat followed, writhing in agony. Almost like one of today's footballers when they fall mortally wounded, only to recover miraculously from the application of the "Magic Sponge". Only in my case, there was no "Magic Sponge"..... but the reaction of the other players on the stage had the same effect.

Elder sister Joey, who was our second mother, was, by now, ready to depart to work, in-service. Murdo, still at school and hating every minute of it, had devised a clever plan to"slip the school" which avoided awkward questions being asked at school or at home.

We would all leave for achool at the usual time but only the boys were "in" on the plan. Whenever Murdo referred to "Coral Island", we knew that another operation was in the offing.The first step was us to assume the characters from R.M. Ballantyne's famous novel – Ralph, Jack and Peterkin. This was the softening-up process and the build-up for the loyalty and secrecy required from the other two, if his absence was to go unnoticed for yet another day. He would stop at the roadside and address Donnie and me thus, "Jack and Peterkin, I must explore the other side of the island. I'll be away for most of the day and you can be on the lookout for my return about 4 o'clock. We will meet at the Pit (this a sand pit close to the road.)

With a solemn handshake to each, he then leapt the fence and, with a parting wave, would disappear into the trees, no doubt with a song in his heart and feeling free as the air. We never failed to rendezvous at the Pit and, as we wended our way home, he would recount his adventures of the day; wandering by the riverside; lying on the banks, watching the salmon leaping tirelessly to overcome the falls and reach the spawning beds.

Although it was many years before Mam and Dad were let into the secret, before too long the Schoolmaster decided that Murdo would be better away from the school. He became an assistant with Willie MacLeod, in his hardware shop at Bridgend.

Donald continued with his studies and in his final year, in the senior class, picked up every prize available. Unfortunately, in those days there was little money available for further study and he left school to become a lorry driver in Sutherland & Mackay's garage.

The banks of the River Shin were very exciting in those days. Hydro dams were unheard of, apart from a small barrage at the end of Loch Shin Water. Fish were allowed "free rein" which made it one of the best salmon rivers in Scotland. On many occasions, on our way to school, we saw so many salmon on the "road pool" of the Rhinamain Burn, that a stone could not be dropped into it without hitting a fish.

Lairg, like the rest of the country, was gradually returning to peacetime habits and, although the Railway Strike, with its hardships, was a serious set back, many pre-war events were resumed. The ewe and lamb Sales had always been an important event in Lairg and was re-established. It was our proud boast, to anyone who would listen, that it was the biggest "One Day Sale" in Britain, with up to 30,000 transactions on the day.

For a week before the big day, stock would arrive "on the hoof", from all corners of the North and West, in some cases having taken over a week on the journey. We often sought out our vantage point at the top of the nearby quarry, overlooking the Shin Valley. We would watch the distant flocks which looked like clusters of maggots, moving slowly along as they approached from all directions. As the sale ring was not far from our home, for several nights prior to the sale we drifted to sleep with the endless bleating ringing in our ears.

On the day of the sale, we were excused school as we were required to fetch and carry water, from the nearby spring at Achiemore, for Miss Mackenzie (Christina). With few facilities, she provided lunches and high teas throughout the day. By nightfall, Christina and her helpers were glad to sit down and enjoy a substantial meal themselves. By then the animals were already moving to the railway loading banks, for special trains which left at intervals throughout the night. By the next day, all had disappeared and silence descended once again – until the next time.

Few cars were to be seen in those days and, apart from the Fords in use by the local Mail Carrier, our car spotting had little reward. I remember only an "Angus Sanderson", a "Bean" and several motor cycles, showing up at the sale. The Highland Games at Dornoch and Rogart were also resumed after the War and there we had our first contact with the "Gladiators" of the day.

Beaton, who hailed from Croy, entertained the gatherings to pole-vaulting exhibitions, clearing some ten to twelve feet. When one considers that his only equipment was a bamboo pole, shoes of doubtful quality, taking off from a field surface that could already have supplied a crop of hay, and without a soft, cushioned landing, this was no mean feat. Hector MacGregor, Spean Bridge, was a well known all-rounder, equally at home with the Hammer or in the Sprints. Starky and the brothers Anderson, are the other "Heavy" names that spring to mind. They were our heroes and many a youngster returned home resolving to emulate them.

Murdo's "wanderlust" had not disappeared with his school books. He was one of several local boys tempted to consider a new life in Canada after attending a film show in Lairg Village Hall aimed at recruiting emigrants. When a decision was required, he signed-on and joined a train for Glasgow bound to embark for the New world.

On arrival, he was one of those selected to help farmers with their harvests. He was very happy there, in the early years, and while things went well, he regularly sent small gifts back to Mam. Before too long, Murdo fell in with a farmer's daughter and on their wedding, the family combined resources and sent a small gift, along with our good wishes. There was simply no question of any of us being able to afford the trip across the Atlantic. Having begun by working for his keep, Murdo was to go on to become a farmer in his own right, renting a relatively small farm in the beginning. Life in Canada was not without setbacks, though.

One day, while working on new fencing, some distance away over the flat prairie, he suddenly spotted smoke and saw that his remote farm house, with only his wife and small child at home, was on fire. He just about died in his rush to get home across the fields and when he got there he found mother and child standing in the open, having only just escaped the flames.The house was completelky destroyed. When the news filtered back to us, in a letter from Murdo, Mam got us to pool together what we could and an, all too small, contribution to the rebuilding of the prairie home was dispatched.

After the Second World War, Murdo's service – he spent several years as a

Forestry worker in Britain in the early 40s – was recognised by the Canadian government who gifted him some extra farm land. By the time of his death, some years ago, Murdo had established his own extensive branch of the Fraser clan in Alberta.

With Murdo's departure for Canada, Donnie leaving school to drive for Sutherland & Mackay's Garage and Margaret approaching school leaving age, our parents had to consider moving, in the hope that employment would be more readily available. With this in mind, Dad had applied for the post of Signalman at Grantown on Spey, which had appeared in the Vacancy Notices circulated by the company at regular intervals. And so it was that, in the middle of June 1925, the exodus took place, and we turned our backs on Lairg, for the more fertile, wooded countryside of Strathspey.

Chapter Two

Grantown on Spey offered many advantages denied to us in Lairg. The Grammar School was, at that time, considered to be one of the best places of learning in Scotland. It was also reasonably near the station which allowed us to go home for lunch. The gym was well equipped, a luxury still unknown at Lairg School and there was an assembly hall where we all foregathered for morning prayers prior to classes. This practice formed a lasting impression that religious studies were the basis of all learning and the roots of Wisdom.

The school also gave us an afternoon break at 3o'clock which was unheard of in Lairg. This difference was the cause of my making the acquaintance of the Rector at an earlier date than might have been expected. On my first day, when the bell went at 3 o'clock, I picked up my school bag and made for home, to find everyone thought I'd been given a half-day holiday. Little time elapsed next morning before the teacher had me report to the Rector. It took me some time to persuade him that the children at Lairg school did not enjoy the privilege of a "little play" in the afternoon.!

It so happened that our arrival in Grantown coincided with the Summer Holidays and therefore that our introduction to school did not take place until we had been finding our way about the town for most of the summer. Odd jobs were there for those willing to work and I began caddying at the Golf Club. I swiftly discovered, however, that the "bob" paid by Mr. Phimister, the Professional, wasn't overgenerous after trudging round eighteen holes, and perhaps only getting a "thru'penny" (roughly 1 pence) tip from the disgruntled players who obviously thought the caddy should have shown more interest in the flight of the ball and saved him some losses.

However, I then landed a job with Farquhar's bakery and worked on morning roll deliveries and bread and cake deliveries throughout the day. Hours of work were seven o'clock in the morning to six-thirty at night for a wage of twelve shillings (60 pence) per week, full time, 8/- (40 pence) when working outwith school hours and full day on Saturday.

At that time, the mails arrived in Grantown at six-thirty in the morning and were carried from the station in a four-wheeled dray with solid rubber tyres hauled by one horse - a desirable form of transport for any youngster. Needless to say, I could always be seen sitting on the tailboard among the mails on my way to work each morning. With the aid of a bicycle fitted with a basket carrier in front, two deliveries of morning rolls on different circuits were made before school at 9 o'clock.

Grantown on Spey was then a small but busy market town, with a good variety of shops and brother Donnie who had already had some driving experience at Lairg, was engaged and became driver on the Tours Bus throughout the summer season. The town was a popular holiday centre, especially for families.

We took some time to adjust to the change from Lairg, as we became less dependent on each other for company and began to find other friends and playmates. Unfortunately, our parents were less than happy with the move. Our railway cottage was in a terrible state of disrepair. The cottages had been neglected during the war and continuing lack of finance made it unlikely that the company would effect any repairs in the near future. Dad decided that the only course was to apply for another transfer, in the hope that wherever they went the housing could only be better.

There was another reason why the move was desirable. The local abattoir was directly opposite.the railway cottages and the custom was to do all the killing on a Sunday. We attended church as a family and respected the Sabbath Day. It was profane, not to say heart-rending, to hear the squealing of pigs and moaning of bullocks all afternoon. Humane killers were still in the future and the slaughtermen used the pick-axe and butcher's steel and a blunt instrument for the pigs. Sheep were laid on a frame and suffered the knife. Some of us were foolhardy enough to venture into the building and on one occasion, as a 'dare' remained to witness the operation – the memory is still with me.

Dad's letter-writing and lobbyings were ultimately rewarded and he arrived home one evening to tell us that we were leaving Grantown to move West, to Kyle of Lochalsh. Our short stay in Strathspey was not all that bad and I have very happy memories of my time in the Scout Troop, under the leadership of Mr. Murray, the postman – of sunny days swimming in the Spey and, on occasions, in Craggan Burn which we would dam to create a fairly good diving pool. During our time there, a traffic census was taken and we spent hours making ticks in a book for each vehicle that passed. When we went absent gathering brambles, we added a few ticks to allow for any vehicles which might have passed unnoticed.

|Kyle was a revelation to us all – the first time we had lived near the sea. Perhaps a short history would help to give a picture of the village which was to become the home of the family for many years – in fact Donnie, Jack and Nan all married and made their homes there.

For quarter of a century, Strome Ferry had operated as the terminus of the Dingwall/Skye railway, before the Highland Railway Company decided to extend the line to Kyle of Lochalsh, the link being completed in 1896. The transfer of the steamer services to the port offered improved facilities and greater harbour space. Many of the merchants who had appeared with the railway at Strome Ferry immediately abandoned the former railhead and set up again in Kyle.
The next 20 years saw much growth. Ferry rights to Kyleakin on Skye were leased to the Railway Company and in turn passed on to local operators. The Railway Company also constructed a substantial harbour for the shipping which was thriving with steady increase of passenger traffic. At the same time, growth of a local fleet soon established Kyle as a busy fishing port.

Railway staff were provided with new and substantial terraced and detached residences, the passengers with a Station Hotel and Refreshment Rooms. To meet the need of the growing population and passing trade of this new village, shop keepers built a grocer's, ships chandler's, flesher's, a chemist, banks and a Post Office.

Kyle still retains some of its original character which was similar to that captured in photographs of early Wild West settlements. The buildings of the main street nestle into cuttings of the rock face. Back gardens perch precariously on the hillside, overlooking the upper floors of the houses.

During the Great War, Kyle became established as a strategic Royal Navy base and the American Army too established an outpost there. By the conclusion of the "War to End Wars" Macbrayne's had confirmed Kyle as an important staging post on their shipping services between the Clyde and the Northern Mainland. Coastlines of Liverpool also joined in, providing the increasingly popular activity of cruising. And that was the picture presented to the Fraser Family when we arrived in October 1925 – the bustle and excitement of this rough rail head the perfect playground for a lad of twelve.

Despite the fact that the rail link now served Kyle and the islands, to all intents and purposes, Lochalsh was still like an island itself, approached from North and South by ferries – at Strome Ferry from the North and Dornie from the South. Prior to the arrival of the railway, Kyle sported only a single building, a Shooting lodge, which in time was to become the Kyle Hotel, which still survives. Balmacara had been the link for shipping, losing its identity with the arrival of the railway and, like Strome Ferry, becoming a backwater.

Fishing played a big part in the life of Kyle. When the summer herring fishing was on, off the East Coast of England, there was a general exodus of women fishworkers from the Hebrides to Lowestoft and Yarmouth.

Special trains were required to convey them to their destinations and they returned in like manner at the end of the season. The Sheila was then the regular Kyle/Stornoway steamer. Though she was able to accommodate the normal number of travellers, this was one of the two occasions during the year when numbers were too much for her. The other being the Glasgow Fair holidays. Then, if the Minch had taken a turn for the worse, she presented a sorry sight, with a hold full of trunks, and miserable passengers strewn about the decks !

With the winter, the shoals appeared in the sea lochs around the North West coast and the herring drifters made their appearance. (Only the mature fish were caught in those days.) Unfortunately, greed was not then unknown and many drift nets were left at the bottom of the sea, full of drowned herring. Often too many nets were set in the first place, with the boats unable to to land any more. At this time, the ports were fully committed, the railheads handling large quantities bound for the South. Kippering kilns were working all out while squads were frantically gutting, salting and packing for export.

Like most villages of the time, Kyle had its fair share of characters but one stands out in my memory like a beacon through the years. He arrived like this. It had just gone 11 o'clock and Mr MacKenzie, proprietor of the Kyle Hotel, had opened the doors of the public bar. As usual, he was busy polishing glasses while the only customer, “Jock Smock”, was already sampling his first dram of the day. At that moment, the door opened and in came Bolton Knott, then a stranger, dressed immaculately in HM Customs and Excise Officer's uniform and wearing gauntlet gloves.

He approached the counter under the appraising stare of “Smock” and ordered a pint of “bitta”. MacKenzie quickly drew the beer and, in placing it before Knott, was addressed as follows. “Are you Mr MacKenzie ?” “Yes,” came the reply. The stranger, with hand outstretched, continued, “Well, I'm Knott !” shaking the hotelier warmly by the hand. No other words were spoken and in the weighty silence, Knott supped his pint with quiet satisfaction, enjoying the first of many in Kyle. On finishing his beer, he replaced his gloves and moved out of the bar. The silence continued but when you saw “Smock's” eyes flickering, you could be sure he was about to speak. With his slight stammer, he addressed the issue, “Wh...wh...wh...who was that Mr MacKenzie ? “I don't know,” replied the bemused landlord, “But he's not a MacKenzie anyway !”

It took a little time for Knott to get into the swing of the place but he was soon to be seen to'ing and fro'ing on his bicycle, with his “Collie” at foot, covering a radius of some 20 miles in the Lochalsh area. His dog was particularly remarkable as it was of a slate blue colour and trained to the last degree. It never left his side. On one occasion, just after his arrival in Kyle, he had the temerity to go abroad one Sunday morning, with a shotgun under his arm and the dog at heel. He was wending his way along the railway line (no trains on the Sabbath) when he was accosted by an irate lady, on her way to the morning service. “You ought to be ashamed of yourself, going about on the Sabbath Day with a gun and dog at heel.” Knott was always the gentleman: “Madam, mind your business and I will attend to mine !” He was, however, quick to learn the ways of the area and was careful to avoid further incidents.

Some time later, it being the first day of summer, he donned his summer uniform of white topped cap, in line with ship's officers aboard passenger and cargo steamers. He was engaged in conversation with a visitor when a seagull chose that moment to relieve itself overhead. Knott was always in control and, with little change in expression, removed his “dress cap” examined it and remarked calmly to the visitor, “It's a good job cows don't fly !”

Soon after his arrival in the village, he became a frequent visitor to the steamer office which, due to the frequency of services, was seldom closed. His regular evening calls were a highlight for a poor shipping clerk who had, then, never heard of a 40 hour week or an 8 hour day. Knott would make his appearance without greeting, take a chair, remove his tobacco pouch from his pocket, choose the correct amount, rub it gently in the palm of his hand, shape it to perfection, wrap it in rice paper and fit it neatly into the bowl of his pipe. Only once the mixture was safely alight and burning well was he ready to talk or listen, whichever was required. We never tired of watching this precise ritual.

John Budge was the Chief Clerk in the local Macbrayne's Agency and he and Knott discovered they had something in common, he having served in the Gallipoli Campaign under the watchful eye of the Royal Navy, which included Knott's ship. They didn't see eye to eye on the way the campaign had been waged but they were worthy protagonists and equally able speakers. They agreed to differ on this issue for the sake of all the other lines of thought on which they were in full agreement.

Knott had joined the Senior Service as a boy and after long service graduated to the exalted rank of Writer. His early service was on a training ship and, according to him, he was given a very hard time by an Instructor who had taken an immediate dislike to him and continued to harrass him as long as he as was under his control. The routine at this time was "strike and stow hammocks at reveille" then straight up on deck and aloft. Knott recounted that if he was up on deck and at the foot of the rigging first, the Instructor would be waiting for him and caned him for holding the others back ! If he was last, he also got caned: "Last again again, Boy Knott ?"

Once, while on Deck Watch, his shipmates were ashore in the local bar, and, when things became quiet and darkness had fallen, Knott thought it a worthwhile risk to slip ashore, have a pint, and be back on board before his absence was discovered. He had had his pint and was in the act of slipping back on board when he was challenged, "Is that you, Boy Knott? Where have you been ? " "I've been here, Sir." "Don't tell lies !" Knott would recount that the Instructor had paws on him like a bear. "Do you know, he brought one round and knocked me bleeding brains out......mind you he was quick, and brought the other one round and knocked them back in again." (All this delivered in a strong Kent accent.)

It was about this time that The North of Scotland Hydro -Electric board were considering extending electricity supplies to the Isle of Skye for the first time. There was much local discussion on how to get it there but Bolton Knott had the answer – build a barrage over Kylerhea Narrows and harness the tides, which at certain periods built up to 14 knots. This, he maintained, would generate sufficient electricity to more than supply Skye.

Knott worked to a timetable which was neticulously maintained and one could set his watch by seeing him at any given point on his rounds. Only once, during his term at Kyle, was his punctuality challenged by a senior officer who was making a random inspection, intersepting Knott at the top of the Colliemore Hill, Balmacara and accusing him of leaving Dornie before time. Knott, true to form, laid his cycle by the road side and, though there were no witnesses to report on what was said, by the time Knott had finished there was one dumb-struck inspector and the Northern Area was minus one officer. Kyle had sadly lost a great character who had lightened the lives of those who knew him. He retired to Rochester, Kent and became “Mine Host” at an inn there.

The primary school, with Headmaster Mr. Montgomery (“Monty”) and two teachers, prepared youngsters for Plockton Higher Grade School but for my pals, Murdo and Callum MacRae and me, it was just a case of putting in time. We were soon to leave school, Murdo to follow the trade of joiner and Callum to become a missionary in Peru and later to be ordained into the ministry. Murdo and I teamed up to become message-boys, after school hours, in the Pioneer stores.

This business was owned by Mr. MacRae, better know as “Old Pioneer” or “Pi”. He had been a very successful business man in the Liverpool area, although he originally came from the neighbouring village of Dornie. When the Highland Railway was busy building the Dingwall to Strome Ferry Railway, he arrived at the rail head and started up in general merchandise. He did very well there and, as soon as the decision was taken to extend the track to Kyle, " Pi" moved there too and carried on where he had left off.

His shop was a veritable Aladdin's Cave but by the time we were assisting he had become less able to manage by himself. Two of his young relatives were given the task of doing the most menial work, while he did the ordering of stock. He spent most of the day on the verandah which he had build to exhibit his wares while protecting them from the vagueries of the West Coast weather. Incidently, the Pioneer was to become the meeting place for all purposes, taking over from the chemist's corner which did not provide such good shelter.

When there was little work to do in the shop, Murdo and I used to be sent up to the garden at the back of the building and on such a high level that it overlooked the two-storey building, being often referred to as "The Hanging Garden of Babylon". "Pi" would set us to work weeding in one section where he had twelve cylindrical stones, eleven of which were always well white-washed and one always left untouched – obviously a Biblical connection.

There was little fertile land in Kyle. The village and station were literally built on solid rock, after it had been reduced to a reasonable level. Much of the soil in the gardens was imported from Ireland at the turn of the century. At that time, many of the fishing villages boasted a few sailing vessels plying between Scotland and Ireland, carrying cured herring and salt out and loading up with soil for ballast for the return trip.

Always a character, at one point "Pi" was admitted to Craig Dunain, the Mental Hospital at Inverness, for observation and became one of their best patients. One day in conversation with the Principal, (who had become a firm friend) he suddenly asked him, "Do you think |I'm mad?" Taken aback, the Principal could only reply, "No, Mr. MacRae, you have been a very good patient who has also become very popular with the staff. As for myself, I look forward to our "daily discussions." Immediately, "Pi," said, "Perhaps under these circumstances you will furnish me with a Certificate to that effect." The gentleman had no other choice and "Pi" discharged himself that afternoon returning home on the next train.

For weeks afterwards, "Pi" was to be seen standing in the verandah and, on seeing any local businessman he suspected of playing a part in having him admitted to Craig Dunain, he would shout, "I am the only sane person in Lochalsh and I have a Certificate to prove it." Needless to say, anyone with a guilty conscience kept well clear.

Commercial travellers as that time were dependent on railways and steamers to reach their customers. They had to have several hampers or cases to carry samples and it was not uusual to see a "traveller" at a shop entrance with his wares spread all over the place, an often futile attempt to obtain an order. It must have taken them weeks to complete their circuit, spending much of their lives away from home and becoming well known. Duff, who travelled for Paterson (footwear,) Sinclair of Hunter Barr (drapery) and Kelly of Rowatt's Tea come readily to mind.

The "Chemist's Corner" was at the centre of the village and the Chemist, Duncan MacPherson, a moving factor in all efforts to improve facilities in the village. His corner window always exhibited the latest news and gave suggestions on how the villagers could assist in improvements. He had come to Kyle to recuperate from a serious illness and had made such a good recovery that he set up as a pharmacist, serving us all for many years. He was a "Progressive" and apart from his work, he found time to prepare and publish a Vest Pocket Guide for the edification of the visitor, which was in use for long years, improved additions appearing at regular intervals. These were a positive mine of information. He was also able to find time to write two books, which sold well, and reflected his love of and enthusiasm for the West.

Street lighting was then unknown, though the Railway Station was lit by acetylene gas, operated by a very antiquated plant which a lot to be desired. While the pier was adequately lit for controlling movement of shipping, passengers had to be wary when moving from platforms to steamer berths. Once a County Councillor, returning from Inverness, on his way to join the Plover returning to Rodel, Harris, had the misfortune of missing his footing in the dark and fell under a moving wagon which was being shunted to another siding. By the time the only doctor, called from a case at he other end of Lochalsh had arrived, a car found to get the victim to hospital at Inverness, and the ferry at Dornie found to be beached because of a very low tide, they unfortunate man had succumbed to his massive injuries.

These were the days when accidents of this nature gave little chance for the survival of the victim. Lochalsh had to face this situation until 1939 and the construction of the Dornie Bridge, hurriedly completed in time to deal with the additional traffic when the naval base at Kyle was re-opened.

Hospital services might have been a long way away but the people of Lochalsh were well-served by Dr. MacRae, at Balmacara. His consulting room was.... wherever he met his patient ! Balmacara, Plockton, Glenshiel, Killillan or Glenelg. He must have been one of the first psychologists, offering to provide a sewing machine to a patient who fell and cut himself with monotonous regularity. Despite his busy life, he still contrived to take a keen interest in the affairs of the area. He was always first choice for Master of Ceremonies at the larger events which always ensured their success. He had a fund of stories which he related between acts and, generally, the audience was in such a good mood by the time he finished that they would listen to anything. He had been an outstanding sportsman in his youth and was capped for Scotland as a Rugby forward. His good lady was also a well-known figure in the locality and they produced a worthy family of one daughter and three sons.

The boys all became fine sportsmen and the daughter was an outstanding curler. Iain, the eldest son, travelled abroad to find his fortune after serving in the army and being badly wounded in the first assault at Cassino. He retired to Australia. Duncan was better know as DJ of St. Andrew's University, Scotland and the “Lions” Rugby Teams. While serving with the Seaforths, he was unfortunately taken prisoner and languished in a Nazi POW camp. Though suffering illness himself, he refused repatriation preferring to serve the needs of his comrades as their M.O. Farquhar, the youngest, also followed in the footsteps of the “Old Man” and graduated in Medicine from St. Andrew's University. Like Duncan, he became an M.O. with the 5th Battalion Seaforths who appeared with the 51st Highland Division in time for Alamein. He continued to Sicily, the Second Front and on to Berlin and victory. The story is told that, during hostilities at Alamien, Farquhar found himself and some “Other Ranks” on the wrong side of the fence. Before the enemy could react, he had acquired a nearby (enemy) truck and with his men beat a hasty retreat to their own lines.

The village of Kyle had progressed much since our arrival and had become a very dynamic place. Many private houses had appeared, despite the limited number of building sites available and the County Council had also build a number of houses. The local Drill Hall, a survivor from the 14/18 War, became the place of entertainment, with concerts, dances and, in time, weekly film shows. The Institute served as a billiards saloon, for public meeting and as a Reading Room. Plans were already afoot to build a larger Village Hall and a very able committee was organised to find the capital required.

On one occasion, the famous Harry Lauder was visiting Balmacara, on a fishing holiday, with an old friend who had retired to live locally. George Urquhart had become a firm supporter of the Committee and broached the subject with Harry, getting the answer “not a penny....but I'll give them a concert.!” and that is what happened. A special train was run from Strathcarron, special ferries from Kyleakin, and the surrounding areas were all represented. The hall could only seat 200 comfortably, so, on this occasion, Harry had to play to 2 houses with only a little support from local talent. It was a memorable evening and brought in enough cash to construct the hall.

Outdoor space was very limited and, though we used a small field for football practice, our home games were played across the ferry at Kyleakin, until such time as a suitable pitch could be acquired or reclaimed from the sea. The pre-war years, however, were full of activities for youngsters interested in sport. A thriving Boy Scout Troop and Girl Guide Company were very active, with the delights of weekend and, ever - popular, summer camps. Cricket, football, badminton, tennis, debating and amateur drama were all on hand. The Drama Club was very popular and always represented in District Finals and latterly in National Finals.Truly it was, a life of "Never a Dull Moment"

Sergeant MacDonald, the local policeman, was a tremendous asset to the village and had all the older Scouts and young men on weekly Keep Fit classes. (None of his pupils ever failed to look after themselves in later years.) He was only one of the many policemen who played their part in the development and progress of Kyle village. The sergeant also trained a memorable Tug-o' War Team who were in full training all summer. Taking part in all the County Annual Games and winning many trophies. There was one memorable incident during training when a crowd of local youngsters were co-opted to get on the other end of the rope and one of them had the brilliant idea of putting a loop of the rope round a fence post. The team couldn't understand how they couldn't master their young opponents and Sergeant was non-plussed too - until he investigated the end of the rope and discovered they were also heaving on the fencepost. The youths were NOT popular!!

I had been out of school a year by this time, having started as messenger in the Pioneer Stores. I was now earning the really quite high wage, for a boy at that time, of 16/- (80p) a week. The years were, by now, taking their toll of "Old Pi" and his niece, Johan who had kept house for him, now began to take charge of the business. Although lacking the business acumen of her uncle, Johan rapidly became a personality in her own right. She maintained control until, in her turn, she was overtaken by illness and had, ultimately, to give up which proved to be the end of the Pioneer Stores.

Johan had developed a great regard for money during her uncle's lifetime and would rather lose in a deal than see a customer leave a shop empty-handed. Naturally, it was not long before the locals cottoned on to this and as a schoolboy, working as messageboy, I used this trait to my advantage. When the shop closed at 8.30pm on Saturday, Johan would make up a package of fruit and sweets and hand it over with a 2/- piece. Even in those days, this was considered a bit below the rate for the job! As a result, I had to evolve some other way of payment and when the opportunity arose, asked Johan, “How long would I have to work to pay for a suit?” She thought for a minute or two before deciding that it would take a fortnight. Thus a new form of barter was born and for the remainder of my time in her employ I was well-clad and shod.

In later years, when I had left school and was established in other employment, I continued to buy my requirements from Johan, always approaching the counter with the maximum amount of cash, I was willing to spend clasped in my hand. If the items produced proved to be too expensive, I would intimate that they were too dear and begin to leave. Immediately my monied hand became a prisoner in Johan's hands and she would prise it open to see how much it contained. As |I always made sure the amount was reasonably close to that asked, a bargain was immediately struck.

One of the contemporaries from my school days was Jim Murchison who was always known as Jimmy the Bear. Now his first job after leaving school was as an engine cleaner on the railway. At that time the loco, which brought in the last train of the day, had to be prepared overnight for the early service out of Kyle in the morning. It had become the habit that, if there was a dance being held in the Village Hall, the engine cleaners coming on duty would prefer to spend some time there before using the long hours of the night to prepare the engine. Not surprisingly, it being a dance, refreshments were taken.

On one particular occasion, the turntable used to reverse the engine ready for its return trip to Inverness, had been examined by an engineer. As they worked on through the night, in the wake of a pleasantly refreshed dance, Jimmy the Bear and his colleague, from nearby Duirinish, assumed that the turntable had been left in the correct position. The result, of course, was that when the cleaning had been completed, the pair drove the engine down to the turntable where it jumped the mis-aligned rails and toppled into the surrounding pit.

In the morning, as the time approached for the departure of the early train, the station staff contacted the signal box asking if there was any sign of the engine. The signalman said he couldn't see it but he could certainly hear it. He was despatched to see what the problem was. He found the Steam Shed empty - Jimmy the Bear and his mate nowhere to be seen- and, with the engine de-railed in the turntable pit, there certainly was a problem. Station Master and Chief Engineer were summoned and a relief engine had to be sent from Inverness before the, by that time, very late train could leave. That night the search for the culprits eventually discovered Jimmy the Bear hiding in a cattle truck but there was not trace of his mate from Duirinish – he had disappeared without trace.

That was the case until a year or so later, when a native of Kyle, who was an engineer on a shipping line trading with Australia, had an extraordinary encounter. A visitor had come aboard the ship one night and asked the Watchman if any of the crew came from Scotland. "Yes" was the answer, "Don MacRae, Chief Engineer." "Where is he from?" he asked. "Kyle of Lochalsh. Just go down below and ask for him." The man found MacRae and his first question was, "How did the Bear get on over the engine in the pit.?" In fact, as it had been judged that Jimmy the Bear had only been partly to blame, he had been given another job, in the Gas House, supplying light to all parts of the port.

Although I was not aware of it, at that time, this part of my life was drawing rapidly to a close, as storm clouds gathered over Europe. One incident from those years, burns brighter in my memory than most. Indeed, nobody in Kyle will forget Coronation Night 1937 when every able-bodied youth and many older men prepared for the celebration by reclaiming an old fishing boat from the beach where it had lain for many years. They loaded her with all the wood-scrap that could be found plus two barrels of tar which had been unplugged and the contents poured over into the hold and onto the deck.

The craft was to be towed out to sea at 9 pm before all retired to the Kyle Hall to celebrate with a Ball. By 9.30pm it had been safely towed out and was alight from stem to stern. It was a magnificent sight. However, those who had been involved in getting the boat out and and set alight could not help being slightly tarred. Many of those who attended the dance didn't get much more wear from the garments worn that night.

Part Two

O'er Heav'n and Earth the Lord God reigns...
but the Western Isles, they're David Macbrayne's.

Chapter Three

Prior to 1870, South West Ross was a sparsely populated area, particularly the Lochalsh Peninsula and means of travel were very limited. In 1853, David Hutcheson and Co., the predecessor to MacBrayne's, had introduced shipping services operating out of Oban to Skye, the North West mainland and Outer Herbrides, calling at many ferry stations en route. The completion of the railway, linking Dingwall and Strome Ferry in 1870, opened up a new link to the West and it was only natural that Hutcheson would provide a linking service with those already operating into Portree from Oban and the Clyde.

The paddle steamer, Mary Jane, had arrived in the area through the good offices of Sir James Matheson, of Stornoway Castle, and Osgood MacKenzie, owner of Inverewe Estate, who were then operating a limited service between Stornaway and Loch Ewe. They sold out to Hutcheson who promptly renamed the the ship Glencoe and set her up on the Strome Ferry/Portree service. By the year 1890, the improved services had opened up the whole of the South West to ready markets and extablished Stornoway as the main fishing port in the North West.

The Glencoe

While discussing Stornoway, perhaps you will bear with me if I digress for a moment. I found this reference to the Isle of Lewis in a copy of the "Thorough Guide Scotland – Part 1" covering the year 1890:

"The late Sir James Matheson and his Lady, assisted by the Steam Boat Proprietors, have been the chief civilisers of Lewis. Her ladyship, we were once told by a resident minister, greatly prejudiced her popularity among the tenantry by supplying their houses with chimneys. There was good reason for this. The Lewis crofter thatched his croft house each year and the old straw, thoroughly impregnated and rotted with its twelve month's dose of carbon from the hearth below, made excellent manure."

I dont know who had the temerity to write this and history does not relate whether he died prematurely while on a visit to Lewis or lived to repent on his misdeeds.

Strome Ferry had now become a busy railhead but the nature of the terrain didn't lend itself for easy development as it was surrounded by very steep hills and sheer cliffs. These continue to offer the danger of landslides, a fact ignored by our modern planners when they constructed a by-pass road to replace the established ferry service. They must bear full responsibility for the landslides which still frequently occur.

The strange tale of the disappearance of the relief vessel, Ferret, will always be part of Strome Ferry history. She was on charter to the operators then serving Lewis while the normal vessel was withdrawn for overhaul and, on being relieved by the regular vessel, sailed, presumed for her home port, and disappeared. Despite lengthy enquiries, she had completely vanished.

Years later, a Lewis emigrant to Australia was working as a stevedore at one of the ports there. While unloading a coastal steamer which had arrived from one of the many islands, with a cargo of hides, he had noticed that although the ship sported another name, her ship's bell bore the title Ferret. He had heard of the ship's disappearance before he left Lewis and he promptly reported the matter. The crew, however, had become suspicious and had cast off immediately and, once again, disappeared. The search was on, though, and the ship was traced to a South American port and Captain and crew interned. Many of them died there and the survivors finally returned to the UK and faced trial. It appeared that the Captain had discussed the matter with his crew and decided to disappear and set up trading in the South Seas.

Strome Ferry remained the terminus of the Dingwall/Skye Railway until the completion of the extention to Kyle of Lochalsh. This was finished in 1896, with the transfer of the Steamer Services to that port which offered the Operators much more space and improved facilities.

By 1928 I had finished with school and was working as a message boy, earning 18/- a week which, at that time, was considered very good pay for a messenger. Work for the school leaver was not easy to get and if anything came up up you grabbed it and hoped that, in time, something better would present itself. Due to this work, I was seldom away from the railway pier, either bringing up supplies to the fishing boatrs or to the Macbrayne's steamers themselves. It was, I suppose, therefore natural that one day I was offered a job with the steamer company. John MacDonald was then Steamer Agent and he made me the offer of clerical work while I was struggling to free the wheel of my "hurley" which had, once again, become wedged in the railtrack which carried the wagons up to the steamer berths at the pier.

Now, I must try to convey the awkwardness of my "hurley". It looked like a wooden liferaft which you often see on a ship's deck but this one had been so badly made that it was decided to fit it with an axle and two gun-carraige wheels, to convert it to a barrow. At each corner it had long wooden legs to keep the carrying surface flat when parked. My legs, on the other hand, were short and each trip with this monster was an adventure, the uneven surface of the cobbles causing one or other of the barrow legs to foul the ground, almost wrenching my arms out of their sockets. I was in the middle of addressing some sharp remarks to the barrow when Mr. MacDonald intervened.

Even then I was very conscious of the value of money and I parried the offer with "How much will I get?" When I was told that Juniors usually began as 12/6, I replied that I was getting 18/- where I was. However, he didn't volunteer any other information so I tried to negotiate by adding that I would be prepared to take his job for 15/- a week. It was left hanging and I wasn't to know, then, that he had made his mind up that I was getting the job. By the end of the week, I was informed that I would start the following Monday and that the Company was, in this instance, prepared to make an exception so that I would get my 15/- . Thus I became a member of the Red Funnel family of David Macbrayne Ltd., 119 Hope Street, Glasgow.

It was an ageing management even then, with the company having been to the fore for 60-odd years. Many of their ships had also aged in the service of the Company. Apart from the normal duties allocated to the Office

Junior, I also became the Manifest Clerk to the then Portree and Mallaig service steamer, Glencoe. She was then of a maturity usually referred to as “her dotage” but she was far from “over the hill”. Unlike modern vessels, she had no Bridge. Her Engine Room Telegraphs were situated on top of the paddle-wheel boxes and the Ship's Wheel set behind the funnel. This last may have obscured the view of the helmsman...but it did keep him warm !

Mr. Latto, the Chief Engineer, looked almost ages with the ship itself and, though, stone deaf, seemed to manage comfortably and was never absent from his post. It was rumoured that to start the engines a punch-bar was required and if that was true then Latto certainly knew where to punch – during her remaining years of service, I don't remember any delay or breakdown. Captain Gilles, who I believe hailed from Kaimes was Master for many years and weighed somewhere in the region of 20 stones, regularly having to withstand heavy weather at the paddle box telegraphs as he manoevered in or out of West Highland piers. Lachie, the Purser, was also an old established servant of the company.

The First Class Saloon was situated at the after-end of the Glencoe and, covered by glass, it gave access to a Dining Saloon on the lower deck. Third Class passengers were confined to the for'ard deck, surrounding a small cargo hatrch and, amidships, a small area of deck around and above the Engine Room. Lackie was very particular that only First Class passengers reached the Dining Saloon and anyone caught Out of Bounds was promptly “Excessed” or compelled to leave his half-finished meal. On one occasion, a County Councillor, on his way to a meeting in Inverness, had the temerity to enter the Dining Saloon for breakfast while possessing only a Third Class ticket. He was duly confronted, in front of other travellers and left the Saloon in high dudgeon, swearing revenge on the Purser.

Poor Lachie wasn't to know that when the Councillor returned from his meeting and, due to a large cargo of wintering lambs, all class distinction was cancelled. The Councellor embarked and took up his position among the sheep. He refused to budge, insisting that Lachie inch his way through the bleating travellers to check his ticket, much to the amusement of the other passengers. Some of Lachie's detractors would have you believe that, when sheep were being loaded or unloaded, he was to be found at the end of the gangway pretending to count the animals but really plucking out loose wool which he would put aside until he had enough for a new suit!

As I explained earlier the Glencoe had been build in 1846, then named the Mary Jane. She was acquired by Macbraynes in 1857 and re-named 18 years later. She operated on many routes and as early as 1890 was on the Oban, Portree, Gairloch service. Many of the crew had spent most of their lives on her and some reached an advanced age before being forced into retirement. No master knew his ship better than Captain Gillies who was seldom seen ashore and who, with his great weight, grudged every trip from his cabin to the controls. The Stornaway Service had been maintained until early 1926 by the Sheila when, due to an unfortunate lapse on someone's part, in the early houre hours of Ne'erday she entered Cuaig Bay, on the north coast of Applecross, at high water and thundered right up onto the beach.

The Sheila

There was little daylight between ship and heather and the unfortunate Master and crew were able to leave the vessel without getting their feet wet, making their way to Milton Post Office at Applecross to report the misfortune. When the tide turned, the Sheila slid back into deep water, thus ruling out the possibility of recovery. Sad to say, though much cargo and furnishings were salvaged, the Sheila remained there and, at low tide, what is left of the wreck can still be seen from the deck of passing vessels.

Captain Colin Shearer had been Master of the Sheila for a number of years but was on leave at the time of the stranding. It was a sad blow to him and, on hearing the news, he decided to retire from the service. He only returned to the area once a year, to visit the Manager of the local Bank of Scotland who, presumably, had continued to look after his financial affairs.

In his day, it was clear that there is no word in the Gaelic to convey the sense of urgency expressed in other cultures by "Man'yana" or "Dopo du Mont". This was the experience of an agitated passenger on the Sheila on passage to Mallaig. The vessel was behind time and " according to the tale" there was some doubt about the ship's arrival before the departure of the Glasgow train. The victim was pacing the foredeck and, yet again consulting his watch, happened to look up toward the Bridge and spied a uniform cap and face sporting a red beard hanging over the dodger and obviously interested in the antics of the man on deck.
"I say Captain, are we going to catch this train?" Captain, in thoughtful mood, looked into the distant view of Mallaig, considered a little longer and replied, "If we don't catch this one ….. we'll catch the next one."

The Sheila, along with her sister ships Plover, Cygnet and Lapwing, was built in 1904. They all provided long and faithful service on their particular routes. It is said that, during this period, the Flowerdale was wrecked and became a total loss, except for the engines and donkey boiler which were salvaged and shared between the Plover and Cygnet.

The Plover

These were days when economies were real and, for example, it was a regular sight to see one or other of the "screw" shipsbeing beached at Balmacara Bay for a keel haul, enabling them to maintain service until a suitable relief became available to allow them to go to the Clyde for their annual overhaul.

Every ship had a few special characters who were out of the ordinary. Many of them had served on the ships for most of their lives and had become synonymous either with vessel or route. No matter where members of the company met, one could be sure that sooner or later the gathering was going to hear a feast of stories, some witnessed at first hand, others handed down.

Such was one about Captain Brown, Master of the Clydesdale, outward bound from Glasgow on a dark but calm night during the winter of 1916. Having just rounded the Mull of Kintyre and debating whether he should follow the rigid Admiralty Instructions, he decided to take a chance and sneak up the Sound of Jura, which would save a lot of sailing time. For the

next hour, they sailed "darkened ship"and were making good time when, suddenly, they were blinded by a sweeping searchlight and challenged by a patrolling destroyer.
Commander: "What ship?"
Brown:"SS Clydesdale, outward bound from Glasgow, on passage to the North West Mainland."
Commander:"What are you doing in these waters? Can't you read your instructions?"
Brown: "Sorry Admiral, it is me who has made the mistake."
Commander: "What's the point in giving instructions if you don't adhere to them? "
Brown: "Oh well, I'm saying it was my mistake, Admiral. I'm sorry, Admiral."
Commander: Stop calling me Admiral, I'm no bloo... Admiral!"
Brown: "Well, I'm saying if you're not an Admiral, ….you should be one !"
It was not recorded who had the last word but one can imagine listeners on both vessels having a little smile and forgetting, for the moment, the cares and discomforts of an active patrol, as lights were doused and both craft melted into the darkness.
The sad loss of the Sheila, as detailed earlier, prompted an interesting story about Captain Shearer from Captain "Charlie" Cameron, from Corpach. He had been relieving the regular Captain on the Sheila just after the tragic and infamous loss of the Iolair, with hundreds of servicemen on their way home to Lewis. During another wild crossing, the servicemen on board were afraid that there was a chronic risk of a repeat tragedy, and appeared to have decided to take over the ship.

Captain Shearer was watching developments from the Bridge and handed over command to his First Officer. He took up position at the Companionway, giving access to the top deck and Bridge, where he was able to repel the first wave by forcibly pushing the men back down the stairs on top of the others. He was able to hold the position and deny access to the upper deck until the Sheila was safely inside the harbour and making up to her berth. He was in no doubt that they had intended to take over his ship.

Captain Peter Grant sailed the dark waters of Loch Ness for nigh on twenty years and had never a sight of the Monster. It was his opinion that, under overcast conditions, a flight of ducks undulating just above the surface set the scene for an illusion of a monster, with humps, moving partly submerged along the surface of the loch. On the other hand, he felt, it could simply be waves created by underwater turbulances which were possible on the loch bed, at the deepest parts.

Captain Robertson was, perhaps Macbrayne's most famous Master, known to all and sundry as “Squeaky” in recognition of his high-pitched twang. Nobody could determine whether he was the younger or elder brother of “Para Handy”. He was the master of the Plover for many years and the two of them had some anxious moments during their many trips together. One such took place while on passage from Tarbert, Harris to Loch Maddy during a severe storm. Under normal conditions, the ship would have been calling at Stocknish Ferry and Rodel but by the time they were off Stocknish they would have settled for shelter anywhere and were, more or less, running before the storm.

The Stocknish Ferryman who had been standing-by on shore, just had a glimpse of the Plover taking an extra big sea and not re-appearing. A telegram was received at Kyle that day saying that she had disappeared off Cluer Point and that it was feared the ship had foundered. However, the Plover appeared at Kyle next day, merely several hours late with its funnel caked in salt and several ventilator trumpets and both companion ladders missing. Later in the evening, the Captain visited the office and when addressed by John Budge thus “You've had a bad trip” the Captain replied, “Yes, we had a bit of a breeze.”

The MacBrayne's steamers,all this time, plied daily to Stornoway, Portree, Raasay, Broadford and Applecross; three times weekly to the Uists and

Harris and every 10 days to the mainland ports in the North West. Passenger accommodation on these ships was very limited but only when the English herring seeason started or finished was the Sheila taxed to capacity.

The Chief Steward on the Shiela at the time spent most of his shore leave otter hunting, accompanied by his pair of Cairn Terriers and with much success. Jimmie the Cook, a die-hard Celtic supporter, was on top of the world as long as “The Bhoys” won. But if Andy McColl's team won (he being Chief Engineer and a rabid Rangers fan) there was open warfare. At times, it made life very difficult for the rest of the Officers and they always hoped that, whatever the result on a Saturday, the fires of passion would be burned out by the time they again took up service in the early hours of |Monday morning.

However, another character, Duncan (better known as Fatty Craneman) who operated the crane on Kyle Pier, was aware of the fragile feelings on board ship. He would exhibit Saturday's result prominently on the side of his crane, just opposite the ship's berth. The Galley was directly opposite the Crane and next door was the passage from the Engine Room. It was inevitable that, as soon as the Shiela tied up, both gentlemen would appear on deck and, dependent on the result, one to gloat, the other to disappear below decks again with renewed fury. Fatty was never present but if one looked around carefully, he could be seen at some vantage point enjoying the results of his handywork.

On the Plover were Christopher Matheson and Alastair Cummings – Christopher, who had fallen heir to a property in South America and who, after deciding ranch life didn't appeal to him, returned to the West of Scotland and rejoined the Company.

Archie Black of the Lochinvar was a household name in the Sound of Mull and a raconteur of the highest order. Archie began service with GJ Burns before joining MacBrayne's. One of his many stories against himself arose from an earlier accident when he fell in to the hold of a ship and, suffering serious injury, was left with a permanent twist to his neck. On a particular morning, the Lochinvar had sailed for Oban and Archie was checking tickets. In the Dining Saloon, he discovered a gentleman having breakfast but whose ticket did not cover that service. Archie promptly recovered the excess and returned to his office on the top deck. Now, this vessel did not boast a very grand office, it being a small kiosk with little room to move. The gentleman had finished his breakfast but was still nursing his wrath. He approached the Ticket Office and addressed Archie while reaching throught the window. "You little B....." he said. "I've a good mind to wring your neck." To which Archie replied quietly, "Don't you think it's twisted enough already?"

The Gondolier

Then there was Ian Aitcheson, of the Gondolier who introduced me to badminton and played the role of "Dutch Uncle" to me in our years together. His favourite story related to a deck hand on the Gondolier who, although a fluent Gaelic speake, had only rudimentary English. One September morning, after an early frost, he had just completed his turn at the wheel and had come off the Bridge seeking warmth on the lower deck. To a fellow sailor, he described this feelings thus : "The fingers of my two feets are as raw as a beef and my two mouses is stuck like a glue with the frost !"

In addition to the normal passenger and goods traffic, dealt with between rail and steamer, the port was kept busy with fish landings. Although Mallaig was beginning to rise in importance, most fishing boats berthed at Kyle, particularly thoses catching herring which were then found in abundance in the Western Sea Lochs. Stornoway was still handling a large quota, both for kippering and freshing.

The drift net was still in use but the ring-net was soon to appear, causing a minor revolution. Some ports, particularly Stornoway, strongly advocated the retention of the drift-net, while Ullapool, Mallaig and many others welcomed the new method which, in time, would destroy the spawning grounds and once again prove that Man is the greatest predator of his own food sources. The stand taken by Stornoway, refusing to accept landings from boats fitted with the new types of nets, in the event sealed her fate as the principal fishing port of the West Coast, and Ullapool and Mallaig increased their facilities and landings with each season.

Improving ferry facilities began to meet the needs of the ever-increasing car traffic and many parts of the West Coast were becoming accessible to the private motorist for the first time. The Company had enbarked on a programme of replacing ships with road transport services. The Fort William/Ballachulish, Inverness/Glenurquhart routes had been extablished as far back as 1912 and now more and more routes were being served by bus. In fact, as many unremunerative services as possible were being withdrawn and replaced by buses and the ships serving on the longer routes were being replaced by larger modern vessels offering passengers and crews a standard of comfort and cuisine unknown previously.

The company's first new bus, a Scottish built Albion.

Chapter Four

With the introduction of the new ships, more thought was being given to tourist travel during the summer season when holiday makers could be offered all-in travel including sleeping accommodation and meals. With this in mind, service timetables were being reviewed, as far as possible with emphasis on daylightr travel. This policy was extended to include other connecting services, railways and road services.

An early example was the 10.15p.m. overnight train from Glasgow Buchanan Street to Kyle of Lochalsh via Inverness, arriving Kyle 10.33am. The steamer for the Outer Hebrides departed Kyle 11.15am, arriving at Tarbet, Harris at 3pm. With the arrival of a new vessel, amendments to service timetables were made and, where most of the day trips were confined to the Clyde, the Oban area and the Caledonian Canal, it was now possible to join afternoon and evening cruises from Portree, Kyle and Mallaig.

One of the most attractive trips intorduced at that time was from Mallaig to Loch Scavaig, where passengers were landed and visited Loch Coruisk. When conditions were right, the view looking to the west end of Loch Coruisk, with the mist rising to leave the pinnacles of the Coolins in silhouette, was breathtaking. The daily cruise from the Broomielaw on the Clyde, to Ardrishaig was still in operation, served by the faithful Columba.

A memorable trip which still warms the cockles of many a surviving heart. No less the Inverness/Corpach cruise via the Caledonian Canal, served by the Gondolier, which offered unsurpassed scenery to the passenger and, whilst navigating the hand-operated locks, a peace and tranquility beyond description.

The Lochness

There was a noticeable change taking place in the make up of the ships crews. In early years, most of the Captains came from the Firth of Clyde area but now the North had begun to produce our Masters. Captain (Squeaky) Robertson, a Skye man, was already established on the Plover and Captain MacArthur, another Skye man, on the Lochness. The Lochness was certainly the jewel of the fleet – oil burning, a rare of speed capable of seeing the boots of any craft likely to be encountered and passenger accommodation that, to the Hebridean traveller, was almost beyond belief.

The Plover was still plying the Outer Isles Service (though her replacement was under construction.) with Captain Robertson and his worthy henchmen – Murdo MacLean, Chief Steward; John Stewart, Pilot; Urquhart, Chief Engineer; and, another worthy, MacDiarmid, Stoker.

MacDiarmid liked to enjoy his weekend breaks at Kyle and on one stormy night, after imbibing fairly liberally, was leaving the shelter of the Kyle Hotel Bar when a strong gust of wind removed his cap and, more unfortunately, his wig. Several minutes later the host, Mr. Mackenzie, came to the door of the bar and discovered MacDiarmid struggling, with the help of a box of matches, to find his cap and wig. Later in the evening a local arrived and asked the landlord if he had anything good to drink on a night like this, whereupon Mackenzie assured him that he had some very good stuff which had blown a man's hair off earlier in the evening!

The Plover and her crew had gained a tremendous reputation for maintaining service under all conditions and no doubt many additional risks were taken to retain this distinction. On one occasion, the ship was on her way from Mallaig to Kyle via Kylerhea in dense fog which had stopped all ships in the area. One of the Kyle dockers had gone to the corner of the pier to see if the fog was lifting. Instread, he saw the shadow of a ship approaching the berth and so close alongside that a crewman was able to hand the mooring rope ashore.

The Glencoe was also on passage from Mallaig but there was no sign of her and when Robertson went to the office and was asked if he had seen anything of the other ship he replied he had seen nothing. The next question was, "How did you manage to come through the narrows at Kylerhea. Squeaky's high pitched reply was comprehensive, "You know, it was a shallow fog bank, lying low on the water and the shepherd at Kylerhea could see our masts above the fog. He was gathering sheep up on the hillside and he kept calling out "You're doing fine Duncan, just carry on." Needless to say the veracity or otherwise of the tale was never established but it is certainly true that no other skipper would have attempted the trickeries of Kyllerhea in such condition.

Many of the well-known vessels were disposed of due to the new policies. The Linnet, which had plied for years on the Crinan Canal, and the Glencoe, the grandest old lady of them all, also went to take her place in history. Built 1844, acquired 1851, retired 1931- a hardworking life of 87 years !

The Linnet

The Plover and sister Cygnet were replaced by the Lochmor and Lochearn respectively, after years on the Outer and Inner Isles Services. These vessels will always be connected with their respective masters, Duncan Robertson and John MacInnes.

They brought to their routes a standard of comfort which had only been enjoyed on the Lewis crossing on the Lochness. Having said that, these diesel powered ships had less exciting lines than their predecessors and, in their early days, had to withstand much criticism from the older generation of seamen. When underway, they seemed to be "down by the head" with the stern appearing to sit up – the nearest analogy being that of a swimming swan. Both vessels, however, proved equal to their tasks, although a lack of engine power was recognised as a big handicap.

Captains Robertson and MacInnes quickly assumed a local popularity which would have been the envy of modern pop stars. In the course of their service, the two ships connected at Lochboisdale each Monday, Wednesday and Friday, with both men meeting in Major Finlay MacKenzie's Drawing Room for lengthy exchanges on the news from "Norse and Souse." On one occasion, the Lochmor was in the vicinity of Canna Pier, enveloped in thick fog. Captain Robertson was on the Bridge while his First Officer was stationed in the bow, peering into the murk and hoping for some break which would give them their position.

Captain to First Officer, “Can you see anything, Mr. Mate,
“No Captain” but I can hear ducks.”
“Can you see if they are walking or swimming? Because if they are walking, we are in trouble!”
In keeping with recorded history, the ducks appeared to have saved the day and, in fact, there always seemed to be something cropping up to protect Master and vessel from accident.

This was borne out on another occasion when the Lochmor approached Lochboisdale Pier with the intention of slipping past the outer berth, occupied by the Lochearn to the inner berth, to discharge livestock which were on board. The tide was well-up and likely to reach the turn within the hour. The vessel failed to stop and gently slid up the only strip of smooth beach within miles! The gangway doors were ordered open and the surprised cattle were driven outboard and wended their own way up the beach. Within half and hour, at high water, the vessel gently slipped back to the inner berth, “without breaking an egg”, as they say,.

In addition to his own prowess, Captain Robertson had his “Man Friday” in John Harvey whose knowledge in seamanship was second to none and who played no small part in the build-up of the Master's reputation. They shared a tremendous respect as weather prophets and it is recorded that while the Lochmor's departure from Mallaig was being delayed by weather, a passenger approached the Captain and drew his attention to a spot of blue in the sky …. Only to be informed, “that's not the direction we're going.”

The Claymore was replaced by the Lochbroom which had previously been the City of London. The arrival of the Lochfyne proved to be another milestone in the history of the Company, the first diesel/electric passenger vessel to be built in the United Kingdom.

The Lochfyne

The Lochness had replaced the Clydesdale on the Stornoway service in 1929. Her arrival had proved to be the beginning of this lengthy programme of replacement vessels, which brought with them a standard of comfort unknown on these routes in the past.

The Lochness, under the control of Captain Norman MacArthur, introduced a new First Officer, "Slasher Watson," who, over many years, was to carve a special niche for himself in the annals of the Company. On his first visit to the Steamer Office at Kyle and being introduced to the staff, he was asked if he was married. He replied in the affirmative, following this up, when asked if he had any family, "Yes, two and one in the stocks." This was a fair indication that we had a real mariner in our midst and he went on to prove that on many occasions in the future.

"Big Donald" was a well known character from Kyleakin who spent his latter days fishing in the Kyle, off his home village. His son, "Tarzan" was equally well known and much of their time was spent trawling for coal around Kyle Pier. This was spilled between ship and pier while bunkering was carried out. On the day of his encounter with the Lochness, however, he was merely fishing after a night of hard frost.

The day had begun brightly with the brilliant sunshine which so often followed in the West. In the early afternoon, “Big Donald” was fishing by handline from his dingy and, being mid-winter, the sun was very low in the sky. The Lochness had just cast off from Kyle, on her way to Stornoway and, probably because of the setting sun, failed to observe the familiar figure in their path. Minutes later they were equally unaware that they had run him down and sunk his boat. The ship travelled on her way for some distance and it was only when one of the crew wat tidying up the mooring ropes for'ard that he became aware of a voice calling for help. Eventually looking over the side, he saw “Big Donald” hanging on grimly to the anchor. A mooring line was quickly dropped to him and he was hauled aboard, much to the surprise of Captain MacArthur and crew. The resulting conversation is not recorded - which is perhaps just as well. Suffice to say that it was near miraculous that a man of already advanced years should survive this ordeal unscathed.

In this same year the Lochshiel, a motor vessel, was added to the fleet and replaced the Brenda on the West of Mull and Loch Sunart cargo service. She was a small ship, to enable her to operate to the small piers and ferrys to be found on this route. The engines could be controlled direct from the bridge but, in time, the Captain was to discover that this was a design of mixed blessing. It was only a great boon until the time came when the engines failed to answer the telegraph, more often than not, leaving little time to make other arrangements. Captain Shearer died several deaths at the hands of this fickle arrangement.

One such occasion saw the Lochshiel coming alongside Islay's Bruichladdich Pier, a difficult quay under the best conditions. The tide was flowing hard, an offshore wind was gusting and the ship approached at a fair speed to offset these conditions. Meanwhile, Captain Shearer was keeping a weather-eye on their position in relation to a submerged rock which contributed to the difficulties of getting safely alongside.

The Lochsheil

At the appropriate moment and under the silent, expressionless gaze of a group of spectators on the pier, Captain Shearer set the telegraph to full astern. The engines, however, were in no mood to answer and the ship continued to forge ahead. Then, presumably breathing a short prayer, he calmly gripped the telegraph and reset to full astern, with no better result. For a moment, he returned the gaze of the watchers on the pier, silently drew his finger across his throat from ear to ear … then frenziedly worked that telegraph as if he was stirring a pan of porridge! Luckily, and as if this desperation action had communicated itself to the wayward engines, the ship finally came under control. Once again, the Master and his ship berthed in safety.

Another vessel, the Denbigh Coast was acquired from Coast Lines and renamed Lochdunvegan, taking up service on the Glasgow/Stornoway cargo route. She had been built as an ore carrier and was an extremely strongly build craft, a fact that the Lochness was to learn by bitter experience. The Lochdunvegan used to sail from the Clyde each Friday and generally arrived off Kyle late on a Saturday night. At this time Captain Lachie Ross, who hailed from Broadford in Skye, was Master and generally took the opportunity to visit his home over the weekend. He always timed his departure, from the anchorage at Kyle, to allow for arrival at Portree when the Mail Steamer had just vacated the berth.

So it was on this particular morning that the Lochdunvegan was weighing anchor, with screw ticking over gently to move her slowly astern but with the Black Ball still indicating that the vessel was at anchor. Either the Lochness failed to give sufficient clearnance, or the Lochdunvegan had indeed been moving astern into her the path, Whatever the reason, those members of staff awaiting the arrival of the Stornoway Mail were startled by a crashing and rending of timbers. The stern of the "Dunvegan" had caught the Lochness amidships and she was staved-in so badly it was possible to look into the cabins on the port side. Appily the damage was well above the water line and the ship was able to proceed direct to dry dock on the Clyde. I need hardly say the "Dunvegan" was always given a wide berth from then on.

This incident may have been the result of a bit of rivalry which became evident when circumstances permitted. In the early career of the Lochness, the populace was frequently wakened by blasts of her whistle when her Master thought that he required more space to make a successful berthing.

All this time Mr. Riach had been Station Master and Harbour Master at Kyle, covering the formative years of the port's development and during the First World War. He was now compelled to retire, due to ill-health and age and was replaced by Colin MacWilliam, a Moray loon who , we were soon to learn, was a Rabbie Burns enthusiast. The MacBrayne's staff were soon to appreciate the occasions when winter storms interfered with the arrival and departure of ships and he was in a mood to entertain us to priceless recitations which carried his listeners away to "The Cotters Saturday Night" and, of course "Tam O'Shanter".

He was to find many worthies within the railway ranks, in particular Jimmy the Bear" whose most famous exploit I dealt with earlier and who fuelled the harbour gas lights at the Acetylene plant...when he was in the mood. One stormy evening when trying to fire-up the navigation light on the pier, he was blown over the side. However, with his desperate call for help, "God save the Bear" and buoyed by his unbuttoned oilskin, he floated long enough for someone to throw him a line. He was a real character.

Sandy Grant, an unforgettable foreman, was a great worker and in one instance adopted a young beginner he christened his "Man Friday", a title which remained with the lad for all time. That lad was my older brother Donnie and the last line of defence in the village football team usually read "Friday, Kirk and Davidson."

The railway station was enjoying the busiest period in its history as Kyle remained the gateway for most of the traffic going to Skye and the Outer Herbrides. In addition to these regular services, we had the Glasgow/Northern Mainland service operated by the Clydesdale which carried only cargo during the winter.

In summer the Claymore came into service for passengers and cargo. She was a beautiful raked ship with fiddle bow and Highlander figurehead, built originally for the Glasgow/Stornoway service in 1881, continuing until 1931. Cruises of 10 day duration were offered in the summer months on this route and there was such demand that a much larger ship would have been hard put to meet it. As it was, berth's were booked in advance up to two years ahead.

Captain Jimmy MacKechnie was the popular Master for many years; Bob MacLean, First Officer, became a top skipper in the Company; William Sutherland, Purser; Matt Pandellus, Chief Steward. Captain MacKechnie limped due to a sea adventure during the Kaiser War and went on the have many adventures with the Claymore. On one occasion, after completing the outward trip at Loch Clash, it was decided to make a quick run to Glasgow. Weather conditions, however, proved very difficult and the trip was completed only after the loss of a lifeboat off Ardnamurchan and some structural damage.

The Claymore

The large dining table was always an added attraction to passengers who had the distinction of joining the Captain at table, adding to the community spirit much enjoyed by “Cruisers”. The Dining Saloon was furnished with a beautiful brass fire and passengers were accommodated in berths situated along both port and starboard sides of the saloon. It was commonly reported that at the end of each trip the passengers lined up at the Pursers's office to book up for a future trip. Whenever the sailing dates allowed, the Captain and passengers spent the weekend at Kyle which meant that the local Church of Scotland congregation had a boost in attendance, as well as Bob MacLean's appearance in the choir.

The Clydesdale, now free of the Stornoway run, was transferred to the Glasgow/Islay cargo service and the old Lochiel became the relief ship, mostly employed on livestock ferrying. On one occasion, she arrived at Kyle with a load of cattle which had been running wild on the Isle of Ensay, an uninhabited Island off Harris. We never heard how they got them aboard there but the ship arrived at Kyle after dark and it was decided to discharge them right away.

Lighting conditions on the pier were poor and it was the practice then to use burning torches. The poor beasts were maddened by the flames and if the reader has ever seen a rodeo and goes a step further and imagines a wild stampede...this was it! There wasn't a pen in the place that was high enough to keep those beasts in and, in any case, those that were available were quickly reduced to matchwood. Searches were mounted to rescue animals that had swum out to sea, others escaped to the hills and many were scattered along the railway track. In the end, several of them were lost, drowned and to injuries which necessitated their slaughter.

The transfer of animals from ship to shore was always a pretty hazardous operation. It was a normal sight to witness a cow in a sling being craned aboard and many, too curious, a sightseer had to make a hurried retreat from the "fallout," frequently failing to make it. On the occasions when there were cattle to go ashore at places served by a ferry, the practice was to push the animals over the side, secure them by a headrope to the stern of the craft and tow them ashore, casting them free when the shoreline was close enough.

Car shipments were few and were mostly dealt with by cargo boats, although the Lochness was well equipped to deal with them. The Kyle/Kyleakin Ferry was also making headway under the control of Mr. Clark who introduced a turntable-craft to handle the constantly growing demand. He had arrived in the area when the then ferry operatores were trying to give up the lease which they held from the railway company. He stepped in and, after commiting every penny to taking over the craft and lease, embarked on a career which was to prove a goldmine, allowing him to retire from business at a very early age.

With the emergence of the new ships and, in many cases withdrawal of steamer services in favour of road transport, it was inevitable that the old ships were disappearing from the scene. Their passing heralded the end of an era. Many of them had operated over their particular routes for almost two generations, with amongst the most notable, the Glencoe.

The Fusilier

It was about this time she was withdrawn from service on the Portree, Kyle/Mallaig service and replaced by a younger vessel......... the Fusilier which had only come into service in 1888 !

She boasted an open bridge with the canvas "dodger" providing the Master and Pilot with some semblance of shelter. However, the passing of the Glencoe left many sore hearts who realised that never again would they see her approaching, with her paddle-box Bridge and the familiar lone corpulent figure of Captain Gillies perched on top, fully exposed to the vagueries of the elements. He remained to command the Fusilier for a short time before retiring.

The Fusilier was a smart ship of some 250 tons gross and proved a worthy successor to the Glencoe. One of her most memorable incidents was the occasion when appoaching Portree Pier on a blustery winter's evening, during a squall, she collided with a wooden fishing drifter, hitting her amidships and slicing almost to her funnel. Captain Lachie Beaton was on the bridge and only his presence of mind prevented probable loss of life. The Fusilier continued to forge ahead toward her berth pushing the stricken vessel before her which enabled the fishermen to abandon ship simply by climbing onto the pier. Captain Beaton had quickly realised that had he heaved-to and tried to disengage the vessels by going astern, it was inevitable that the doomed vessel would have sunk immediately and, on such a night, would have put the lives of the drifter crew at great risk.

The changes in the fleet continued and by 1937 the Lochness, Lochinvar, Lochearn, Lochshiel, Lochfyne, and Lochdunvegan had been joined by the St.Columba and King George V replacing the Columba and Iona in that order. The Lochgarry replaced the Lochbroom, the Lochgorm was a spare ship while the Pioneer continued on the Islay service and the Gondolier still plied the Caledonion Canal Summer Service. All these changes had taken place within ten years and there was now a fleet of some 23 ships, as well as several smaller ferry craft.

It was about this time that I was being called upon to stand-in for Pursers who, for one reason or another, required to be away from their posts for short periods. Port Managers were never too enthusiastic about a member of staff performing these relief duties, as past experience had taught them this was often the early sign of the permanent transfer of one of his staff to a job afloat!

The St. Columba

Chapter Five

The Fusilier on the right, tied up with the Glencoe.

My first introduction to sea was as temporary Purser on the Fusilier, which was then serving the Portree/Kyle/Mallaig service and coincided with the Glasgow Fair holiday. The regular Purser, John Noble, had suffered a bereavement in his family and so, far from getting any instruction, I was met at the foot of the gangway on the steamer's arrival at Kyle, handed a bunch of keys, and left in charge.

In those days, the Glasgow Fair was the one period of the year when every ship on the West Coast routes was crowded beyond capacity, or should I say beyond beyond certificate! As my first day was a Friday, I had only to deal with those small numbers who were fortunate enough to get away a day early and avoid the crush. Saturday was THE day. In Mallaig the trains from Glasgow arrived in three portions and the pier took on the appearance of Hampden Park at the end of an International. Notice boards were sited at strategic points directing passengers for Stornoway and Kyle to board the Lochness and those for Armadale, Glenelg, Raasay and Portree to join the Fusilier. The bulk of the cargo traffic was handled at Kyle, so most of the stuff loaded at Mallaig consisted of the usual suitcases, prams etc and little time was lost in getting everything on board.

By this time I was installed in the Purser's Office, ticket window open, and calling all passengers for Armadale requiring tickets to come and get the. It was a short leg across to Armadale and one had to look smart to get all the fares collected. It was only on an occasion such as this that you realised how many Skye men were employed on the railway, the Clyde Trust and other forms of Glasgow City Transport ,which entitled them and their offspring to priviledged travel on steamers!

It proved a hectic baptism for me and it seemed only minutes had passed when I was issuing more written-privilege half tickets for Glenelg. I was able to get a bite of lunch while going through Kylerhea and was better prepared for the next influx of passengers joining at Kyle. If this was my "longest day" then I hardly noticed it, so much had to be done with so little time to do it. Most of the weekend was spent preparing Returns and thankfully, with the assistance of George McIver of the Portree staff, a balanced Return was submitted on Monday morning.

This introduction to a Purser's life was soon followed by a trip on the Outer Island service, on the Lochmor, relieving Alistair Cummings who had gone south to attend a wedding. At that time, the ship sailed at 6.00am on a Wednesday morning and it proved to be one of these exceptional mornings when a following southerly wind was light, and, blissfully unaware of my good fortune, breakfast was taken while we passed through the Sound of Rhona. Everything was going fine and, by the time I had gone over the ship's manifest and listed seperately the cargo to be landed at the individual piers and ferries, we were aproaching Scalpay Harris, our first port of call.

Scalpay had a good sheltered pier, except when there was a westerly gale. On one such occasion, the Captain had decided against making the attempt to go alongside and instead lay-off and signalled for a fishing boat, which was sheltering at the pier, to come out and take off several local passengers. The fishing craft was fully decked and offered little shelter for the passengers, who, by the time the craft had made the pier, were thoroughly soaked. They were also of the opinion that the Lochmor could have got alongside with little risk.

When the Lochmor returned to Scalpay on her next trip and was easing alongside under the command of Captain

The Lochmor

Robertson, the local minister, who had been one of the unfortunates on the previous trip and who was obviously still smarting from the soaking he suffered, was on the pier and on the attack as soon as he knew that the Captain and anyone else interested could hear. “They tell me, Captain, that you could easily have come alongside on Wednesday, and I may say that is the general opinion.” There was a silence for but a moment as the Master ensured that his ship was almost there. Then with a dangerously calm demeanour, he gazed down at the poor mortal,...and replied, “They tell me that thon sermon you preached on Sunday was trash...but no doubt you were, like myself, doing your best."

On this occasion, however, Scalpay was cleared with little time lost and Tarbert, Harris, our next call, was just across the way. The weather, however, was rapidly changing, with the balmy southerly of the morning having backed to southeast and heading for a real blow. After leaving Tarbet we managed to clear Stockinish Ferry but by the time we were off Cluer Point the ship was just managing to keep her head into a heavy sea and speed was down to a few knots.

I had already parted company with my lunch, and in fact tomato soup has never tasted the same since ! I was having great difficulty in sharing my time between the bucket, and issuing tickets. It went something like this: ticket window down, issue ticket, take fare - window up – bucket - window down – the motions repeated as the situation prmitted. When the last passenger had been dealt with, I had to lock my cash drawer to prevent it sliding out and depositing all the loose cash on the floor. Or rather, to prevent it happening a second time!

I had to lie down on a bunk to get some peace and, as kindly Emma the Stewardess brought me another cup of tea, I could only hope that this time it would stay down. The trip remains in my mind as one of the poorer experiences of my my life. It was made worse by the fact that, on arrival at Lochmaddy, the ship turned about and crossed to Dunvegan, returning again to Lochmaddy before continuing on to Lochboisdale. I only survived the experience thanks to the help I had from the stevedore, Dan MacGillvray and of course the nursing of the Stewardess.

Thus I discovered that this type of life was not for me, although I was determined to avoid amy risk of losing advancement in the job due to refusing to go to sea. This resulted in another uncomfortable experience. It was a hard life in those days for a Purser whose only chance of getting away from the constant movement below his feet was when the annual holiday came around. More often than not, though, he had to wait until the

Company found someone who would agree to carry out the Relief.

After my first experience, further requests were less readily agreed to. But in an emergency, someone had to do. So it was in the following instance. James Ferguson who had recently joined the Company on his return from a post in West Africa, had arrived to take over from John Campbell, the then Purser of the Stornoway steamer, who had been taken ill. The weather was anything but good and for the first few trips the Lochness faced a nor' easterly, and anyone who has been at sea under similar conditions off the "Shiants", knows full well what it can be like.

Poor Jim had a miserable baptism and resorted to the "crater," which may help one to forget but, added to sea sickness, leaves one the worse for wear. The result, of course, was that I was pushed out again. Just to prove that there was no ill will the wind continued from the same quarter for the next week! However, I had discovered that if I issued and checked all passengers and tickets and locked all cash drawers before the ship passed Rhona Head, and retired to my bunk, I could weather it out and be fit enough to have my tea after arrival in Stornoway

Jim had taken my post at Kyle Office but was still feeling far from well when he showed up, and someone suggested he should visit the barber's and spruce up with a shave. The barber greeted him and asked what was wrong. "I'm fed up" he said, continuing, " and I'm going to drown myself.""Why bother shaving?" He was asked. "I would like to look respectable when they find me." Needlesss to say, Jim did nothing so drastic and continued to serve in the Company for some years, eventually becoming hardened to the life of a Purser.

Lochness served on the Stornoway/Kyle/Mallaig service from 1929 to 1947. Only on one occasion in 18 years did she fail to make the trip and that was due to the herring fishing fleet setting their nets at the entrance to the Stornoway harbour, and the Master, then Captain Norman MacArthur, refusing to sail until the nets were cleared. She was the first product of the plans to modernise the fleet, built by Denny of Dumbarton and oil fired. Her speedy crossing of the Minch soon created a need for an earlier departure from Stronoway and a general speed up of connecting rail services for the South, both at Kyle and Mallaig. Soon other ships began to appear including the Lochfyne, the first diesel/electric powered vessel and the first in Britain, for the Ardrishaig winter service and summer cruising. The Lochmor and Lochearn for the Outer and Inner Isles service. The Lochshiel arrived on the Sound of Mull and Loch Sunart cargo service to the exclusion of the Brenda. The Fusilier was also soon to be replaced on the Portree mail service by the Lochnevis - another outstanding product of Denny's. This vessel could take off from any pier like a sprinter and for the first time the Lochness was shaken from her perch

The Lochnevis

and no longer was able to have her way. It is true though that on a long leg the Lochness could make up the leeway lost at the start. However, the Master of the Lochnevis would see to it that as soon as the other vessel was getting too near, he would change course and maintain that he always ordered a change of course at this point. Some of these occasions proved as exciting to spectators on shore as it must have been to those on board, especially when the leading vessel boredown into the path of the overtaking one. From then the outcome depended on a strength of nerve. Captain MacKenhnie, a native of Inverness, became the Master of the

Lochnevis and continued there until his retiral.
By this time the whole of the shipping services were undergoing changes and after many years of valuable service to the Western Highland, David MacBrayne, had decided to call it a day. He was then receiving Government Assistance to maintain the service but he had intimated that he was not going to apply for a renewal of the mail contract. His intention was circulated to members of staff throughout the Company and all employees within six months' service and over were given a sum based on years of service.

David MacBrayne's retiral was indeed the end of an era and many stories are told of the man which portray a character that could only be found on the Western Seaboard. In the early days of his management , it was well known that he avoided engaging non-productive workers, and only hired auditors when he set out on a duty tour of the agencies and ships of the fleet. He generally started by joining the Columba at the Broomielaw, which resulted in a chain of telegrams illicitly sent and arriving at all ports with the simple message “The Bee...is on the Wing”. Despite advance warning some pursers failed to check and, dependent on the extent of the discrepancy, suitable punishment, including at worst dismissal, was meted out.

There is one story told that when he arrived on board ship his presence was not immediately observed and a shortage was discovered. On leaving the ship MacBrayne saw his quarry on the street and made a point of stopping him and giving him notice that if he saw him again in the area he would have him apprehended and charged by the police. The story goes on that he did not see his ex-Purser again on that tour but saw him again the following year and renewed his threat to such good effect that the purser wasn't seen in the area again...but was last sighted in Sydney, Australia.
In the early days, when the ships returned to the Broomielaw from the outports, both the Purser and Chief Steward, after completing their cast returns, brought them up to 119 Hope Street, where MacBrayne sat at his desk and checked the takings personally.He then asked the purser to

produce his wage list and the chief steward his catering requisition. From the pile of sovereigns, he extracted the sum required and then pulled open the draawer and swept the residue in, stating, "This is mine". His system of accountancy had a lot to be said for it, with the profit margin requiring little working out and it didn't matter a hoot where it was made, as long as it got into the right drawer. He must have been an outstanding person as, when he handed over the business, he left behind a staff to whom MacBrayne's had become a way of life. It is perfectly true that to be a member of the Company earned anybody a welcome whereever they appeared in the West of Scotland.

No other body had been interested in takaing over the services, and it had been only after a direct appeal from the Government that L.M.S. Railways and Coast Lines of Liverpool came together and formed a new Company which became David MacBranye (1928)Ltd. There was still little change in the ships on service: the Clydesdale on the Stornoway service; the Plover on the Outer Islands; the Glencoe on the Portree service; the Claymore on the North Mainland; the Lochinvar on the Sound of Mull; the Cygnet on Inner Islands; the Pioneer on Islay; the Columba to Ardrishaig; the Gondolier on the Caledonian Canal; the Linnet on the Crinan Canal; the Brenda on the West of Mull and Loch Sunart cargo; the Lochiel on Islay cargo; the Iona on Staffa and Iona cruises; and the Mountaineer operating short cruises out of Oban.

Now ten years later, the situation in Europe in November 1938 had already persuaded the Government that, despite Chamberlain's triumphant return from his visit to Germany, war was inevitable. In years to come we would realise that the Prime Minister's convincing "Peace in our Time" covered up a realisation of the imminence of conflict. Appeals were made to strengthen the Territorial Army and many companies were to make concessions to staff in order to attract volunteers.

David MacBrayne Ltd acted, and many members of staff, including me, joined up locally. Naturally we were mustered on 31august 1939, having attended a summer camp earlier in the year. We had been assured that attendance at camp would not curtail salary and that, if called to regular service, our salary scale would be maintained, less the sum received from the army. Exxperience was to prove that those who gained promotion soon saw the portion paid by the Companay relentlessly wither away, soon ceasing altogether. This perhaps reflected the low level of salary being paid prewar.

For me, this was to result, at a time when mail from home was taking a long time to catch up, in my receipt of a letter from the Company Accountant advising me that I might find time (!!) to repay £100 which had been overpaid. Of course, the Company contacted the Army Pay Office, and continued to do this at intervals to avoid any overpayments, ultimately leaving it all to the Pay Office and ceasing to contribute altogether. This was despite the fact that they were paying their ship's crews War Risk Bonus in addition to normal salary! I suppose these anomalies were bound to arise but considering the coastal conditions in which these crewmen were serving, it left those on active service feeling rather bitter, to put it mildly.

War news was being carefully monitored and as expected those who had answered the Company's call to arms and who had attended the summer camp had been forewarned that there would be another later in the year. The call came on the afternoon of Thursday 31 August. Those involved busily got their work up to date before reporting to the local drill hall and made their farewell to the Company.

The events of the next few years is another story and in only a few instances was I to make contact and hear of the goings-on in MacBraynes. One of them occurred on a cold wet January morning in 1941. It was an early hour in Gourock and I was one of the troops boarding a transport that was lying alongside. On proceeding down the gangway who should I spot but "Bunty" MacDonald, First Officer of the King George V. As an honoured guest, and to the envy of my comrades-in-arms, I was invited to the Captain's Table for breakfast. Captain Bob MacLean was well known in Kyle and a popular figure. I remember he and Mr. Kindness (Postmaster) entertaining at the Church Social, singing the "Flotsam Midsummer Duet" - very effectively too..

But back in August 1939, our future was anything but certain but I had few qualms, despite recalling the happenings of the previous hostilities. I was now a man of 26 and was soon to discover that my experiences over the years with the Boy Scouts and Rover Scouts, together with the periods of training under the able control of Sergeant MacDonald, with his keep-fit, boxing training, added to weekend camps and hill climbing, fitted me out to overcome all difficulties. In fact, the experience gained from camping in the bad weather and generally adverse conditions of the West Highlands enabled me to keep wartime difficulties, even on active service, in perspective.

Part Three

The Left Handed Gun

Chapter Six

Volunteer and Veteran, 1994

Dingwall's Ferintosh Distillery was no doubt a suitable property for distilling the Water of Life but it certainly lacked many of the requirements for a comfortable army billlet. It had been hurriedly divested of its usual furnishings of butts, hogsheads and casks to increase flooor space for our use. The accommodation on offer at Ferintosh was not quite up to our expectations - concrete floors, steel doors etc.- but our standards were to experience some drastic changes before we were very much older.

Christie Boy – A MacBrayne's Man

Our call to arms had been made a week before and we, the 5th Seaforth Highlanders - regimental tradition recruited from Wester Ross - had been standing-by at the village hall, pending movement instructions to proceed to the battalion area. Early that morning we had entrained at Kyle and had continued to pick up sections at all stations serving the Wester Ross area.

I was fortunate to find a corner in the storeroom which was to serve as Company Office and Senior NCO's sleeping quarters. I, as a poor private, realised that the only reason for my presence there was to look after the Office and become dogsbody for all those entitled to use it. This new way of life was difficult to accept for most of the boys and myself in particular. It was made more difficult by the attitude adopted by a small number of NCOs who, in donning the mantle of authority, discovered a new found power which others found difficult to thole.

Ablutions had been erected outside the building, with only a canvas windbreak to protect against the elements and anyone unlucky enough to be taken short during the night had to be fully dressed before venturing out. You can be sure that this situation held many a trap for the unwary who had to partake of food prepared by cooks who were yet to be found out. It was a common sight to see some poor soul glued to the box and suffering.

I had one such miserable experience, coming awake at some early hour in agony and by the time I had got into some clothes, zero hour was almost upon me. With every retentive muscle working overtime, I was shuffling rather that walking. As already mentioned, the doors were of heavy steel and some thoughtless person had closed them fast. They were mounted in the wall and reached by a short set of steps. Several times I climbed the steps but each time I was unable to exert sufficient pressue to open them without the risk of an internal explosion. Sergeant Alex MacKenzie, laying awake and enjoying the spectacle, finally relented and, " I passed him like a flash and disappeared into the darkness."

The month wore on and colder weather had set in making it more uncomfortabel than ever to wash and shave in the open, though more shelter had been provided for the sit-down jobs. Training went on apace and we were gradually moulded into shape, becoming more hardened to this new way of life with readier acceptance of the discipline meted out.

Humourous incidents in training abounded and I can still see a lad taking a "sighter" with a rifle resting on the T.O.E.T. stand, wearing an eyeshade because he couldn't shut one eye without closing the other. It was his own idea after getting a bit of ribbing the previous day. It was amazing to see the changes that were now apparent in the bearing of the individual and one could detect a quiet confidence in the quietest mannered fellows, no doubt the result of endless periods of instruction.

Many of the Easter Ross and Dingwall lads were still able to nip home whenever they were free from duties but those hailing from west of Garve had to make the best of their free time in the town. We didn't do so badly. The National Hotel had become the Officers' Mess but the Royal Hotel was still available to us and we often made our way there, when we were flush, sure of a slap-up meal. In fact there was a very pretty waitress there, a charmer from Gairloch, whose presence ensured that we would soon return whether we were flush or not. There was another angel, who like Lochinvar, came out of the West and, now residing in Dingwall, had become established at the Railway Station, serving teas etc. to the troops passing through. Her home became an open house to us and if the town of Dingwall ever considers erecting another memorial in Station Square, let it be in honoured memory of Rebecca Shearer.

Now that the early training stages were reaching their peak, most of the platoons were as near to full strength as possible. Those less fitted for square bashing had been found other duties - ie mortar platoon, pioneers, cookhouse, transport and clerical staff duties. I had already learned that, though considered an A1 recruit, I was permanently unsuitable as an infantry soldier because I was left handed. It was therefore inevitable that, as a shipping clerk, I would find myself posted to the Companay Office. So for me there was no great change from civvy street, other than my days now being wholly filled by Pay and Mess Rolls; Kings' Rules and Regulations and Clothing Vocabulary; Parade States, including Strength Returns and Battalion Orders. At least I was doing a job for which I felt qualified but it took me a long time to get out of this rut and find something more to my liking.

The time had now come for the Battalion to move South, to join up with the remainder of 154 Brigade. On a day in October, we entrained at Dingwall station amid a crowded turnout of the populace to wish us Godspeed. The Division, including the other Brigades, was to concentrate in the Salisbury Plain area and we were directed to Inkerman Barracks Woking, for the next stages of our training, with a marked improvement in facilities and comfort. Woking was well used to catering for the Services and we settled in quickly, resuming training where we had left off. During our off-duty evenings, we soon discovered the good places to visit, with the "Robin Hood" roadhouse providing a popular choice for us - a discovery which we kept very much to ourselves as long as possible.

Training now took the form of regular route marches, patrols, guard duties and lengthy exercises on Salisbury Plain. Firing Courses were carried through on Bisley Ranges and. though many of us were becoming reasonable shots through practice, some of our gamekeeper lads could still show the rest a thing or two, particularly when it came to snap shooting. Duncan MacLennan, who hailed from the Attadale area, was out on his own and to witness an assembly of officers in the Butts, to be shown his handiwork, must have given him great satisfaction.

On the other hand, the only person interested in my shooting prowess was Sgt. Major Anderson who, on seeing me shoot off the left shoulder, bawled me out. "Get that rifle on the other shoulder", I replied (still in the mood to kick against the pricks), "When I'm using this weapon against the enemy, you will not be present and after all it will be natural to fire from my best shoulder...SIR". Fortunately, he did not pursue the matter. In other ways, though, I made my mark by preparing a companay shooting detail, displaying an individual shooting table of placings within the Company, which promptly saddled me with the task of completing a similar table for the battalion.

Reinforcements had been reaching us these past weeks. In the first instances Seaforth Reservists who had been recalled to the Colours, and then a strong contingent of Militia Boys from the Royal Scots Fusiliers. These young lads took some time to settle, no doubt finding it difficult to understand the "Teuchtars" from the Highlands, who it must be admitted were a clannish lot. But these were early days and the time was soon to come when these same lads, from the Lothian coal mines, proved that they had few equals when digging revetting trenches.

We were now undergoing inoculations and dental inspections, and there was a general feeling that we would soon be on our way. However, out of the blue, we had an outbreak of German Measles which we promptly renamed "Goebels Trouble" and I, in company with a lot more, found myself in isolation. As soon as each individual was pronounced clear, he was bundled off on Sick Leave, failing to realise, however, that in fact it was embarkation leave, with all measles victims becoming the Rear Party when the Main Body in turn went on Leave, over Christmas and New Year. In my case it was doubly unfortunate as, just prior to contracting measles, I had decided to visit the Barrack Barber and requested a short-cut. Before I realised his understanding of short cut, I was left with a very short stubble and so, being sent on Sick Leave, it gave me quite a thought. I was the original Skinhead and wasn't too enthusiastic aboutmaking such an appearance in Kyle.

Sergeant Alec MacKenzie (Dash), Privates Chisholm and Fraser moved out from Woking for London in the afternoon, to join the overnight train fore Inverness. On arrival in London, we quickly shed our kit, including arms, leaving them in the charge of the left-luggageman. This was a practice which in later years was considered unpardonable but we were yet to learn. Our next objective was somewhere to feed and a notice inside the door of a Voluntary Aid platform canteen, advertising bacon, egg and buttered bread, had immediate results. We enjoyed this meal...repeated three times each ! Once the hunger had been satisfied, and with still time on hand before the departure of our train, we wandered down Euston Road, where the noise of sliding bolts on a bar front was enough to furn our steps toward that quarter.

It was our luck to meet three London businessmen who, it appeared, made a habit of meeting there for an aperitif before going their seperate ways. You can imagine our delighted surprise to be served with a large Scotch each, with their compliments, which of course, brought us together. It was no surprise to learn that they were all members of the “Old Brigade”, and by the time they helped us on to our train they were in the mood to join up again! In fact the train had to be held up to let them off.

We were in holiday mood on boarding the train, sharing a compartment with some naval personnel on their way from Portsmouth to Scapa Flow. They were naturally in less happy mood and we commiserated with them. At the first stop, Chisholm promptly nipped across the station platform and managed to buy a half bottle of Scotch at the buffet bar. This we shared with our naval friends, who in turn produced some bottled beer, thus ensuring a happy, and restful journey to Scotland. My appearance at home caused a few raised eyebrows but they soon got used to my short haircut.

I noticed a great change in Kyle - most of the shipping using the port were service vessels and almost all residents of service age were either away on service or under orders. Our family were almost all involved, Joey (V.A.D.) Jessie (Q.A.), Donnie and Jack (R.A.S.C.) Murdo (Cannucks). The latter had been in Canada since 1924 and the set-up was kind of similar to “Beau Geste”, the only difference being that there was never a “Blue Sapphire” to go missing and provide us with an excuse.
Donnie already in France and the others scattered over the U.K.

It was always a treat for me, when I came come on Leave, to be able to bring Dad a rare dram. For many years he had been the Precentor (the leader of the unaccompanied singing) in the Free Church of Scotland. But when I was home on Leave we would have a Dram, and then he would sing, in Gaelic, “Caberfeid”, the song of the Seaforth Regiment. I didn't understand the words, but it was one of his great favourites. In later years I was to discover that, in his younger days when still working in Lairg station, Dad had been very fond of the occasional dram.

One member of the Skinner familay, for many years hoteliers in the Lochinver area, told me he had got to know Dad very well on his many trips south, via Lairg. On one occasion he arrived there to catch the early morning train on New Year's Day. The train was very late, so he went in search of the warmth of the office. His version was that he found Willie McCrost playing the accordion and Dad with his boots off and performing the Sword Dance, Mam's version, at least as she told us, was that there had been a hard frost and lots of ice on the steps at the signal cabin, which were very hard when you father fell down them. We had noticed at the time that she seemed to have had “many words”with him.

The Leave passed quickly and I was soon on my way South again, leaving earlier than necessary to allow some time to give London a look over. The train arrived early in the morning and I was soon delving into that bacon and egg breakfast which had given us so much satisfaction on the way north. I intended to buy a wrist watch, believing that if any place could provide a good buy, London was it. After humping my kit across London to Waterloo station by the underground and again disposing of it at the left luggage, I sauntered out to have a look at the Big City.

In no time, I was inveigled into buying a watch considered to be the best available but which, in fact, proved so unreliable that I committed it to a watery grave, through a porthole somewhere in the English Channel, not many days later. Even then London was living up to its reputation;I had already parted with some cash to help a lag who told me he had just been released from the “Moor” which for all I knew might easily have been the Moor of Rannoch. As I proceeded down the street, going toward Westminster, I was again accosted by a stranger, enquiring where I was stationed and the unit I was serving with. We had been well warned about careless talk etc. and, though he appeared to be a reasonable type, he was not going to get any help from me.

He promptly produced his Life Membership Card of the Seaforth Regimental Association, at the same time informing me that he was Donald MacLennan, Commercial Artist, residing in Freshwater Raod, London. We immediately became firm friends and he gave me a wonderful day in the City in his company. I left him with his promise that if I was able to get a weekend leave while in the area I was sure of a welcome at his home. Unfortunately, time didn't allow for another meeting, but memory of that encounter will always remain with me as one of those cherished surprises that one meets within a lifetime.

I rejoined the Company at South Guadalupe Barrracks, Bordon, that evening and was to learn that many changes had been made in my absence. Ages and in some cases Birth Certificates had been

Christie top left, Seaforths, 1940

checked and those under age had been reposted back to the Depot at Fort George, near Inverness while some inter- Company transfers had also been made. C/Sgt MacKenzie had gone to Headquarters and C/Sgt Matheson had succeeded to our Company. Arrangements were well ahead for the Battalion going on leave and I, along with others just returned, became the rear party, assigned to keep the wheels turning while the main body were away.

It was all go and, though we were disappointed at missing leave over Christmas and New Year, we made the best of it. I had arranged, when at home, to be sent a good supply of "salt herring" to arrive in time for Hogmanay. The package duly arrived and, before we adjourned to the licensed canteen, we put the herring in a zinc bucket, along with half -a-stone of "Tatties" which I had earlier purchased from the NAAFI.... much to everyone's surprise.The party decided that each spirit order would be doubled and the bottles containing ginger ale would, after use, be filled with spirit and secreted away for carrying back to the billet - we were learning fast! Midnight found us congregated in our billet, seated on the floor, and feeding from individual sheets of newspaper containing two salt herring and a puckle of boiled tatties in their jackets In days to come, the tale of that supper was to be retold many times and in strange places.

No sooner had the battalion returned from leave than final arrangements were afoot for the move to France. SD Tunics, kilts and trews had been exchanged for battle dress, and pay and mess rolls had disappeared in favour of field acquittance rolls. The early hour of 18th January 1940 found us on our way to Southampton, there to join the cross channel steamers; in our case the Daffodil and the Rose of Tralee. It was one of my more exciting birthdays!

Lord Haw-Haw had already broadcast to the world that "the 51st are on their way but there is a cold reception awaiting them in the Channel." We didn't get cold but he did force us to return, delaying our departure for a few hours. The crossing gave us more palpitations than the enemy did, being somewhat rough, but we safely arrived at Le Havre and were soon on our way to Bolbeck, some twenty kilometres away.

We took up residence in some outbuildings belonging to the chateau on a large estate. Here we were to experience the most severe winter conditions. Personally, I have never known their equal. The forest trees were bursting with frost and the continual noise sounded as if a battle was in progress. Telegraph wires, subjected to freezing rain, became several times their normal thickness and the sheer weight pulled the posts down. Much of our time was taken up with tidying up the grounds and providing plentiful supplies of firewood for those lucky enough to have somewhere to burn it. Our outbuilding had a concrete floor and sometimes it took all your strength to prize your boots free after being left on the floor overnight.The Baron, however, was kind enough to lay on a "grog party", which helped to stave-off more serious results.

We were now entering the "Phoney War" and we were not yet committed to the Forward Defensive Lines in the North, no doubt due to the extreme weather conditions prevailing which made it impossible to move freely. Much work was yet required to improve those positions and it was no surprise to us when the order came through to move north by rail rather than by road. We entrained at Bolbeck, being allocated good vans with doors left ajar to prevent suffocation, thus repeating the experience of a previous generation.

After a slow and weary journey, we arrived at "Wingles" and "C" Company were directed to a disused factory which , to say the least, was in a dilapidated condition – outer doors had been removed presumably to allow for the transfer of machinery, and never replaced. In the prevailing hard weather, it didn't offer much comfort and a concrete surface to sleep on made one feel cold just by looking at it. The factory's previous occupants had been a unit of French African Troops who kindly left behind a scattering of straw which was promptly utilised to protect bodies from the cold floor. A glass panelled office situated in the centre of the floor space became the Company Office. It had been the Overseer's obsrevation room and with a wooden floor gave us a warmer surface to lay our heads.

In the course of the next couple of days, it was discovered that the straw was infested with lice and practically everyone in the Company was carrying more than their fair share. To avoid more serious consequences, prompt arrangements were put in train to procure a mobile fumigation boiler and have a clean-up. The boiler dutly arrived and the lads were lined up and ordered to divest themselves of all cover, down to the buff, and stood there while all their garments were committed to the boilder for purification. How we survived the experience, despite the extreme cold, still seems a miracle.

Despite the misery, there were some lighter moments too. The Medical Officer decided to take this opportunity to include an FFI Inspection. Duff, an old soldier had a body liberally tattooed, including an eye on each cheek of his posterior. In the course of his inspection, the MO was heard to exclaim, “I've examined many an arse but this is the first time I've found one looking back at me!” In the meantime, the building was thoroughly cleaned out and the straw fired and, though the lads were subjected to increased cold, they at least slept without a scratch.
Our sojourn in Wingles was not to last much longer and we were soon on the move again, this time to Lilliers where we were to take part in defensive work to fill the existing gap between the Maginot Line and the sea. The whole area of the Belgian Frontier was wide open, due, we were given to understand, to the wishes of the Belgium Government. Lilliers proved to be a welcome change from our previous quarters and billets were made available to us in the village. Company Office was was set up in one of the local Estaminets, clean and comfortable and some of us were billeted with a local family.

Four of us were allocated an attic bedroom, reached by a ladder which, need I say, was removed once we were bedded. I had no fault to find with the lady of the house for this system as she had a very desirable daughter who required looking after.The old lady had experienced the occupation force of the previous was and no doubt was well aware of the dangers attending young hearts thrown together under similar circumstances.

The only real disadvantage facing us was the risk of being taken short in the period when no exit from the attic was possible. One of our party, a bit longer in the tooth that the rest of us, and known to us as “Boots”, was a consumer of large quantities of French beer and according to him it didn't remain within the body anything as long as English beer. It followed that he was always being caught short after we had settled down for the night. Not being able to reach the ground floor, it was inevitable that the jug and basin which had been provided for washing facilities became his private storage chambers.

Everything seemed to combine to prevent us from disposing of the contents of these utensils during daylight. Severe weather had again set in, bringing heavy falls of snow and very keen frost, with the result that the only skylight was buried deep in snow and iced up. This made it impossible for us to get rid of the amply stored liquid which now took up the full capacity of a chamber pot, ewer basin and jug.To crown all, it was discovered that the liquid had now become solid ice. The situation was rapildy becoming desperate, with the threat of a billet inspection due any day. This crisis lasted for two more days and, on the Saturday night, with a billet inspection on the morrow, desperate remedies were being considered.

We had reached a decision to cover the nearest bed to the skylight with a couple of gas-capes, to protect it from the falling snow that would be loosened when we opened the skylight to jettison the offending liquid and ice from the over-full pot. But unknown to us, French airforce lads, returning to their camp near at hand, had spotted the light in a downstairs room and, as far as we could make out from the landlady's rather expressive method of explanation, chose the very time to call when we were disposing of our waste from the skylight directly above. There was an immediate uproar but, after we bellowed a few well chosen Scotch greetings, the strangers departed.

The old lady seemed well enough satisfied with the outcome and, when the time came for us to be on the move again, she gave us a party on our last evening. A sumptious meal was laid on, although we didn't relish much the taking of the rabbits from the hutch at the rear of the house as well as the pigeons from the loft. A liberal quantity of wine and brandy was had by all and true to her age, Madame entertained us with songs from the Old Contemptibles, correct in word and verse. Before leaving, we had a rise in temperture resulting in widespread flooding but thanks to the Highlanders, sandbagging helped in no small measure and damage was limited.

It was in these better weather conditions that we moved to Roubaix and were again billeted in the town. The Company Office was sited in a substatial house which was very comfortable. It was the property of a local doctor who for some reason, made it available to the army. Working parties from the Company moved out each day to dig and revet trenches and rumour had it that ultimately the Division would take over a section of the Front. It was hoped that, in the event of the invasion of Belgium, their Gevernment would open their frontier to enable us to advance to defensive positions on the Albert Canal, in an effort to slow down the enemy attack.

This plan failed to materialise, however, and by 28th March we were again on the move, to take up Divisional positions on a line between Bailleul and Armentiers and our Company settled on a farm about four kilometers east of Bailleul. The outbuildings and the steading lofts were reasonably comfortable. The Office, as usual, was allocated the best available which I considered made up for many of the other restrictions suffered by those working too near the fountainhead.

We had made a long jouney, in a long time, and on arrival we were in the mood to eat a horse, which turned out to be near fatal. The cooks had tried to be clever by opening all the tins of McConnachie's stew the night before

and bulking the stew into the hay boxes. On arrival, all that was required would be to heat them up and the meal would be ready for serving
It ws done with the best intentions but we were all soon to learn that you don't treat tinned stew that way. The stew was devoured but within an hour or two the majority of the Company were suffering from a fairly acute attack of Ptomaine poisoning. We were rested the next day but it was a lesson learned and not repeated.

Patrol work was undertaken all along the frontier, in conjunction with the the French frontier guards. For the first time, I was included in this work and I relished the chance to get away from paper work and be with the lads. The presence of the police made the job more interesting, especially on these cold mornings when they knew where to go to get an early coffee well laced with good French rum. It fairly warmed the cockles of our heart.This period, though quiet with us, was in fact the prelude to the onslaught which descended upon us like an avalanche within weeks. Fortunately for me, although I didn't think so at the time, the die was cast that I would escape this catastrophe.

The Company had received a set of barber's clippers and a volunteer had been found to treat some of us to a haircut. My crop had, at long last, grown in and I was the first customer. Though the barber was willing, there was still a bit he had to learn and while he finally succeeded in shearing my locks it was only after many nicks, particularly on the back of my neck. We were, at the time, sleeping up in the hayloft and, possibly with the help of some dust, I quickly discovered that my neck was being assailed by some virulent infection.

For some days, I tried to forget about it, hoping it would go away but in the end I had to visit the M 1 Room, where bad fortune still lay in wait. The sergeant applied some concoction which proved to be highly toxic and, by the next morning, I was in a sorry state, with a temperature of 103 degrees. Within an hour I was stretchered away to the nearest first aid centre. My arrival there seemed badly timed, as the Medical Officer and Dental

Officer had planned a night out and, though the medical officer appeared to be conscious of my need of special attention, he was easily persuaded by the DO that, with the aid of pain killers, I would be alright until the morning. Their conversation took place beside the stretcher which was to be my bed for the night.

At about 2 am I was aware of a light shining into my eyes. This heralded the return of the two revellers who, in their hazy state of mind, thought I should be examined again. Sitting up on my stretcher, I was looked over by both officers. The state of mind of the MO required a lot of re-assurance from the DO, the former now being of the opinion that I should have been evacuated to a Field Hospital that night. As the unit was on twelve hours' notice to move, he would have little chance to complete the transfer first thing in the morning. The DO reasoned with him that if he had a patient to evacuate, his unit would have to notify Brigade that they would be unable to move before his job was completed.

Finally, they wandered away to their quarters, leaving me to dose away until daylight, glad to be left alone. I doubt if these officers would ultimately have made the grade. Despite these vicissitudes, which dogged my journey from one Camp hospital to the next, includjng travel by hospital train, I finally arrived at the City of London General Hospital, Boulogne, to be reassured that real hospitals did exist with clean white sheets and angelic nurses. My troubles were not over, however, and despite heroic efforts by the nurses I worsened to such a degree that no specialist consulted could discover my trouble and I became an aoutcast, moved intoisolation. No-one could possibly feel as down as I did then. Indeed, I feel I had fallen victim to my worst ever ill wind and it blew bleak and chill as the German Army was reported on the move through the Low Countries. I knew that, very soon, comrades would be committed to battle, while I and other patients were unfit and unable to play our part with them.

Meanwhile, moves were afoot to evacuate us to England and while the 51st

Highland Division moved from the Maginot Line to the Belgan Frontier, I was stretchered aboard the hospital ship St.David ahead of an incident free passage to Southampton. From there we entrained for Prestron Hall, Maidstone (British Legion Home) which had become a casualty Dispersal Centre. After several days, I finally arrived at Queen Mary's hospital, Sidcup, which coincided with reports that the 51st Highland Division had been cut off, with little hope that they could be extricated from this position. It was later confirmed that they had surrendered and been taken prisoner of war.

This was the final blast of the cruel ill wind, which left me in a very distressed frame of mind. I had yet to realise that, just as all previous ill winds had blown some good, so had this one, providing me with an escape from the prisoner of war camp and like the cruiser Glasgow Colonel, I lived to fight another day.

Chapter Seven

On arrival at Queen Mary's Ward 15, I was greeted with a cheery buxom nurse's, "Come with me, Jock. I know what's wrong with you !" For the next two hours, I became her sole concern as she performed a very difficult and painful shave, and spirit wash , before completely masking me in saturated lint. This was treatment with a difference, and for the next four days the same procedure was followed. Each day, when the mask was removed, everyone was convinced a miracle cure was being performed. A special diet of fish and chicken, no doubt, played a part. In any case, the world was returning to being an interesting place again, though the war news was anything but bright.

While in France. I had been having a bit of bother with a torn cartilage in my right knee. On many of the route marches, the thing had kept slipping out and had now become like the sneck of a gate, requiring little encouragement to dislocate and doing so regularly. It was common for me to be observed sitting at the roadside pushing the cartilage back into place. It was quite painful to do this, but once re-set I could continue what I had been doing, although the knee was never free from surplus fluid. This disability had become such a part of every day life that I ceased to consider it anything other than a "blooming nuisance.".

Now that my recovery to rude health was only a matter of time, I began to take an interest in other activities and I used to consort a lot with a "Geordie", who occupied the next bed in the ward. I may say we were two of a kind and, inevitably, we finished challenging each other and being a nuisance to all and sundry. We had a Battery Sergeant Major in charge of the ward and he became so exasperated during one of the daily arguments between the Geordie and me, he addressed me thus "Jock, you're the only Scotsman in the ward and you make more noise than all the others put together." Mind you, I thought he was biased, he was from Durham.

The day came, however, when the Geordie boy thought he'd have a laugh at Jock's expense. We were sunning on the lawn in front of the ward. The lad had always tried to impress the listener with his feats in wrestling and did seem to know all the different grips, etc. He suggested I become a pupil and he would demonstrate a "scissors". I was always the type who innocently accepted these moves, and too late, after he had me firmly wedged, I realised he was going to enjoy this. I quietly suggested that he had proved his point and should now release me but instead his enjoyment was so acute that he continued to apply the pressure. My patience was exhausted and my pride in ribbons. As I fought my way free, the picture resembled a couple of tom cats having a go and it took almost the rest of the ward to separate us and restore order.

It was some minutes before I discovered that, in the frac, my cartilage was well out and was unusually difficult to replace. Sister had already given us the sharp edge of her tongue and we were to appear before the senior officer in the morning. I was still trying to get my knee unlocked when she returned to the scene and had me sent back to the ward. An orthopaedic doctor was summoned and promptly replaced the cartilage. He again visited me next afternoon and on re-examining the knee suggested I should give him a demonstration on how to put it out. Innocently I refused to do it, saying that it was painful enough trying to get it back without deliberately putting it out.

I was always slow on the uptake and it took me some minutes to realise that he thought that I was making the most of the cartilage business. Being me, I had something to say about that. I reminded him that I was a Volunteer who had joined the army in 1938 and rather than put up with a damaged knee, I wanted it repaired to allow me to return to active service as soon as possible. He took me at my word and the following week I was moved to Surgical Ward 3 to prepare for the operation.

Ward 3 was a friendly place and, though I continued to visit Ward 15, I had now found a little nurse from Orpington. "Little Audrey" was a delight and being of that name suffered many cracks linking her to the character who was very popular during that period. It was a great pleasure to be her assistant on ward duties, such as preparing the afternoon teas and dishing out endless supplies of cherries, which were so plentiful that summer, appearing in some form at every meal.

The day came when Lambrinudi, a Harley Street specialist, performed a perfect operation and I came-to plastered to the hip. The German anaesthetic "Heavipan" was then in use and , as far as I remember, I had counted to three before passing out. Apparently I counted to nine but then, after everything had been prepared, I suddenly said "Ten"! Consternation reigned. "He's coming out, keep him under with ether!" I passed out at 8.45am and came to at 8.45pm. All afternoon the theatre team and others had been round my bed trying to bring me round. Jack Cruickshank, from Aboyn, told me they were even playing with something under the bedclothes! However, when I did eventually waken, I felt as if I had been drinking ether all day and was violently sick. Even to this day I cannot stand the smell of ether.

To be confined to bed was a new experience for me. I could never bring myself to ask for a bedpan and it was only with secret movements that I would condescend to use a bottle. This attitude got me into many difficulties. As the pressure mounted after three or four days, I decided to tackle the difficulty in my own way. During the quiet period in the afternoon, I would gradually push my splinted leg towards the edge of the bed and thereafter borrow crutches from the lad in the next bed and make my way to relief from there. All went well, except that my gammy leg had been pushed too far and fell to the floor and the wound was badly jarred. However, I pushed on and had almost made it when the ward began to revolve. I had to drop the crutches and grab the nearest bedrail. The cry went up "Nurse, it's Jock" and I was promptly bundled back to bed, still unrelieved.

The Exercise was only delayed for twenty four hours, when another attempt would be made to reach that coveted "throne." No stupid mistakes this time. With the asistance of the headrail of the bed, I would gradually pull myself upright before making any further move to leave the bed. Unfortunately, I hadn't thought about the lamp above my bed, and, in my final struggle to become upright, my head had come in violent contact with lamp, globe and shade. Immersed in broken glass, I didn't dare move my foot. I was very unpopular with the ward staff and my secret was finally out. In any case, I couldn't hold on any longer and, much to my embarrassment, I was forced to adopt an undignified position behind the curtains screening my bed – and with very bad grace.

Little time was wasted on getting me on my feet again, and on the seventh day the splints were removed, stitches taken out and I was walking by the afternoon. The following evening, I managed to join the boys at the local and listened to Winston making his famous speech of defiance. We all walked tall on the way back to the ward that evening. Another week and I was taking my farewells and heading north for a short leave before reporting to Fort George.

Much had happened in the meantime, and I had to have a special pass to enter the Kyle area. The port was now a busy naval base and it was astonishing to see a balloon barrage around the loch, as well as AckAck and coastal Batteries nestling in the hills. News of the rest of the family was that Donnie had escaped from France, getting on board a trawler with a few others and safely away. On arrival in England, many of the escapees were despatched on a short leave until some order could be restored, as records were very incomplete.When Don's 48 hours had expired and he had left to report at his RASC Depot in England, a telegram was received from the War Office informing us that he was posted missing and believed to be a prisoner of war.

Jack ws serving with the RASC. in Norfolk. Joey was a VAD Nurse (naval section) at Lennox Castle. Jessie was a nurse with QA's and Isobel was in the post office. Nan was still at school.
Naturally there was little to keep one's interest after hearing all the news of the family and I was soon ready to be off again. I reported to Fort George in August, where I was informed that I was to be posted to Depot Conpany, on light duties, pending a medical board with a view to downgrading.

I soon discovered that light duties included coal fatigues and many other similar unpopular tasks. Depot Company was so disorganised that nobody was very sure how many men were on the strength. There was always a full complement on pay day but in between times numbers were very much less. Those who were left soon became disgruntled, being so frequently on Rampart Picquet, which lasted for a full week at a time. I had already made contact with several friends from the 4th Battalion who had also been lucky enough to have been lightly wounded or ill in the early days and evacuated before the Panzers cut the routes to the ports. My old CSM was busy collecting survivors from the 4th Battalion, to add to the strength of the 5th Battalion but, being aware of my pending medical board, refused to include me on his list.

This period was the least interesting of all my service. It was an old established barracks full of "old soldiers" jealous of their cushy jobs, who spent all their time and energies finding work for others to do. Some place had to have the distinction of being my pet aversion and this was it. It was to witness my first experience in crime, which of course creeps up on one so unexpectedly.

On our arrival at Fort George, our Army Pay Book No.2 was withdrawn and forwarded to Army Records, Perth, and, in most cases, was brought up to date and returned. But my book hadn't shown up again, and all enquiries made to trace it proved futile. I have often wondered if I should write them again, just in case it has since come to hand.

My friend, L/Cpl Alec MacKenzie, was more fortunate and, when his book was returned, he was delighted to learn that he had a fairly substantial credit. We discussed this matter seriously, realising the danger that they might change their minds before we were able to make the most of the situation. A suitable story was concocted and my friend's financial situation after pay parade was so healthy that he agreed we should get late passes and make for Inverness.

The Carlton Restaurant was still the best in town and we indulged ourselves with the choicest morsels available. We were still wet behind the ears, so our new found opulence went clear to our heads. It was decided to book a couple of beds in the Soldiers and Sailors Home and attend a dance at the Cameron Barracks. In the meantime, we met two Canadians whom we entertained for a while before proceeding to the dance. We had just got there when Alex remembered he was duty NCO i/c Dining Halls next morning, which entailed being there at Reveille. The arrival of the first bus was not until much later. The last bus for the evening had already gone and there was no other course open to us but to start walking the ten or twelve miles between us and barracks. We didn't mind the prospect but only then did we remember that we were on late pass and would certainly not be back in time to get through the Guard Room and book in. Worse was to come, though we failed top appreciate it at the time.

We had reached the Nairn/Ardersier cross roads and were having a quiet smoke, when a heavy vehicle approached. This turned out to be a bus returning to the Barracks after delivering the Dance Band to some function in the Inverness area. It duly pulled up and we were soon having to lie low between the seats while the vehicle negotiated the South Gate and preceeded to the vehicle lines. We promptly sprinted across the square and were in our bunks in record time.

Reveille brought us back to life and I ws suddenly conscious that the Orderly Corporal was calling my name and number. Apparently, I had already been called, just after midnight, and faialed to answer the call. I was on my first charge - "absent from 23.59 hours until reporting to Orderly Corporal at Reveille." For the first time, I learned that it was an advantage to be a Lance/Jack and only a Private was exposed to the extreme ravages of King's Rules and Regulations. I reported to the Orderly Sergeant who gave me the feeling he had been waiting for the moment and, like Rabbie's Jean, had been "nursing his wrath to keep it warm".

We were lined up and, as soon as my turn came, he literally threw himself at me and I got the feeling that he was foaming at the mouth. Every one of the utterances flayed me as if I was exposed to electric shocks and, as I moved "at the double", my Balmoral was plucked from my head and hurled to the ground. That was too much and I almost committed myself to the worst of all punishments - the Glasshouse. I stood before Captain Mitchell, who read out the charge and, on being asked if I had anything to say and attempting to say something in my defence, I had my second lesson - "the accused has never anything to say". I was marched out , had another tongue lashing and the second performance went off without a hitch. I was confined to barracks for seven days. I was learning the hard way and the corners were gradually being chipped away. Although I was in a hurry to leave Fort George, we had our lighter moments and so far there had been no further word of the Medical Board.

It was about this time we had our first Emergency Call out. It happened on a Saturday evening in early September. Alec MacKenzie and I had gone to Inverness and to the pictures. There was a sudden interruption to the programme and a message flashed on screen for all Camerons and Seaforths to return to their respective barracks immediately. On emerging, we discovered that all the local buses had been commandeered and put at Army disposal. We were quickly conveyed to Fort George to find everyone on "standby" and so we remained until stood down on Sunday morning. We were never very clear about what was the cause, although rumour had it that some German Transports had been detected and then attacked in the North Sea.

It was never my intention to become a "Base Wallah"... but I also had no intention of committing suicide. In one of my more adventurous moves, however, I happened to pass the Detail Board and noted that volunteers were wanted for something or other. I said to myself, "Why not me?" On entering the Orderly Room I spied a previous antagonist, Cpl. MacFarlane, with whom I had crossed swords on one or two occasions, particularly on the question of ot being included in the draft for the 5th Battalion. I had to be aggressive and so the following conversation took place:
Me: "Please add my name to the list of volunteers for special duties, Corporal".
He: I thought you wanted to go to the 5th Battalion ?"
Me: I'm like you Corporal, if there is a better job going, I'm for it."
He: I don't think jumping out of aeroplanes is a better job - will I take yourname off?
Me (with a lump somewhere between my throat and chest) "No, leave it on".
Exit volunteer, with blood draining from face.

Details the following morning included instructions for Private Fraser C 2822017 to report for interview at 11.30am. There were five volunteers and by the time it came to my turn I was was much less brash, knowing now what it entailed. The usual standard questions - "Do you have a car or motor bike?" - negative. "Do you swim?" "Very short distance." Examiner remarks - “At least you're honest. You will report to Orderly Room 9.30 am tomorrow for Movement Orders.” This was to be my farewell to Fort George Infantry Training Depot, with no regrets. My MO came to hand and I proceeded to Brechin to join No.11 Scottish Commando, who were then training in that area.

This unit was to last for almost two years and the varied roles played by this independent Brigade during that time could rightly be described as “Never a dull moment.” The other Commando, making up the Brigade, were Nos.7 and 8, both of them recruited from English units. The 11th Yeomanry was composed of troops from all the Scottish Infantry and Yeomanry Units, which of course produced intense competition, each troop vying with the other in training and in the end producing a highly trained unit.

Each Commando was composed of ten troops of fifty men, and made up generally of 3 officers, 9 NCO's and 38 Other Ranks. Instead of Sections, we had Parties, consisting of Bren Gunners, Bombers and Riflemen. The training was strenuous but I think the feeling abroad at that time, in the army, was to “Get on with it.” If you didn't like it, you weren't allowed to hang about and many of the lads found themselves on their way back to base very quickly.

Most of the troops were billeted in private households in Brechin, which were given extra rations to help satisfy the extra appetites. But, by the time |I arrived, there were no private billets left and I joined other late arrivals sleeping in the Cathedral Hall and feeding in Gillatly's Restaurant. One thing I am certain of is that no-one was better fed than I, and those with me. Mrs. Gillatly, a gem, contrived to keep the bakery business going, along with the restaurant and it was there that I sampled my first Forfar bridie.

On one occasion, we were out on a full day scheme and of course were famished with “Haversack Rations”, made up of two bridies and a few parkins. The bridies didn't last until the meal break, having been consumed within an hour of setting out. This resulted in a hungry horde descending on Gillatly's in the evening. Thankfully, second helpings were always available. My taste buds still thrill to the memory of the stews served there. It would be facinating to know how many of those lads survived the war and returned to Brechin to pay homage to that wonderful lady and her restaurant. I did and I believe others went back and stayed.

Our Commanding Officer, Col. Peddar, of the Highland Light Infantry, gave full rein to his imagination in organising training, so that much of it was quite different to that laid down in official manuals. On one of our numerous night ops, he observed a Bren Gunner hesitating on the bank of the fairly deep river. On enquiring, he was told that the Gunner doubted the river was too deep to get across without wetting the gun. Whereupon the CO picked it up, threw it into the middle of the stream and remarked "You have no doubts now."

There was much freedom afforded us, when off duty, and when a rest day was granted it was an initiative test for some of those with homes within a radius of a hundred miles to get there and back within the time. This practice almost caught us out very badly on one occasion. We were all on a Rest Day, and Movement Orders arrived unexpectedly, giving little time to prepare for the move. The "Fiery Cross" went out, covering an area from Aberdeen in the North to Glasgow and Edinburgh, Dundee and Perth. We paraded ready to move at 2200 hours, entrained and away by 0130 hours. There were no absentees and nobody queried how they got back. I believe a Dispatch Rider, in some small town, visiting the Post Office had left his motor cycle on the stand, engine running, and when he came out it was gone and later found abandoned in another hamlet - near Brechin!

Our train arrived at Gourock some hours before daylight and we boarded a tender which was to take us to some larger craft at anchor in the Clyde. As we all trekked across the gangway, I had a real surprise to see the Chief Officer by the gangway wearing the familiar MacBrayne's colours.

Bunty MacDonald was an old friend and the "King George V"a favourite craft. The old ship had already played her part, having made three trips out of Dunkirk. I believe that, for the first time, she carried more that her compliment - on each journey - but I don't think anyone complained. Captain MacLean (Big Boab) Master of the "King George" was the Commodore of the Fleet, and he kindly arranged for my release to join him at breakfast.

We were soon on the move and alongside the "Royal Scotsman" which was to be our base for a few weeks while we were to take part in combined operations around the Isle of Arran. We were very comfortable, two men to a cabin and sharing ships duties with the other troops. We felt, at that time, that we may have been intended for Norway but due to the early collapse, and evacuation there, this was knocked on the head. While the ship had sustained some damage recently, her visit to dry-dock was delayed to permit assault training. However, the facilities available were not satisfactory. For example, the lifeboats were too clumsy to be used for night landings and it was no surprise when we got the news that we were disembarking at Lamlash and the ship was to proceed to dry-dock for repairs.

The 11th Scottish had already been to Arran for a period prior to my joining them and, as then, we were billeted with those locals who could undertake the job of feeding us. It was a tremendous experience, and Mrs Shaw, Brodick Brae, did us well - a home from home. Training became noticeably more rigorous and the pace increased......so did the number of failures, disappearing quietly back to other units. Various types of craft were used in training, including canoes and wooden lifeboats. These were a bit better than those of steel which had proved impossible to get off a bouldery beach.... if some careless guard failed to note the ebbing tide.

Every corner of the island was visited at some time or other and one of our first tests was to march up the Stirling Brae and across to Sliddery, returning by the coast road to Whiting Bay and into Lamlash, non-stop. I remember the day well as some of us had been visiting our local friend Matthew Kerr, who owned a gift shop situated at the head of Lamlash pier. He and his good lady lived above the shop and we already had a very successful code in operation whenever we had occasion to be near the pier. As soon as we heard the knocking on the front room window, we knew the tea was ready. It was then up to those in the know to find some reason for disappearing.

On the night prior to the march we had been able to procure a bottle of rum, which we had shared with Matthew and it was a bolt out of the blue to find we were on a march at short notice. There was little trace of the rum by the time we had toppped the Stirling Brae, although there were distinct signs of first wind difficulties. It was normal practice, on a route march, to travel fifty minutes and rest ten in every hour so it was therefore anticipated that a break was due any minute. However, time and miles passed with no change and we were soon consulting our watches for the packed lunch break. When 12.30 arrived we got the message, "Anyone feeling hungry should eat now - we are not stopping."

By this time, we had built up a strong comradeship, closest being the members of your particular Party, and, in my case, they were Davy Gunn, from Wick and Joe MacArthur, from Greenock. Others were equally loyal to their troop and formed the earliest specimens of the irregular soldier, with unorthodox training, highly competent in the use of arms, explosives etc. and ready to play a part in any theatre of war during an emergency. Jack Collins, a cockney, and Rocky Stocks were two outstanding characters. Collins had been a time served soldier with the HLI and, following his discharge, was a docker at Bermondsey Docks, before volunteering at the outbreak of hostilities and becoming a Commando.

Each troop had been issued with an anti-tank rifle, which weighed thirty eight pounds. During his time on the docks, Collins handled a great deal of timber and had developed what they used to term a "Big Shoulder". He was ideally suited to carry the Bois Anti-tank Rifle and it never ceased to amaze me to see him place the rifle on his shoulder and march for miles, with never a thought even to transfer it to the other shoulder.

We had many humorous episodes involving Jack, especially when we were getting instructions to climb some precipitous coastline or traverse rough ground during a trek. On one occasion, we were negotiating the Goat Fell Saddle and had to cross a stream which had lots of flat rock, festooned with green slime, which any hill walker will confirm can be a dangerous trap for the unwary walker.

Jack's attention must have been diverted at the crucial moment of crossing and he landed heavily in the burn. We had been subjected to a good going Scotch drizzle for the previous two hours so it wasn't the wetting that annoyed Jack but that the Anti-tank Rifle had followed him down and jammed his fingers on the rocks. Even Goat Fell veiled herself in mist to avoid the unusually choice language ricocheting from peak to peak. Captain Blair interrupted the flow and suggested Jack get a grip of himself ! Silence prevailed except for the "squelch, squelch" of boots sinking into and sucking out of the peat bog. We had just crossed the Saddle and were faced with a descent over a steeply sloping grassy patch when Captain Blair, in the lead, was suddenly careering over the ground on his posterior, with his kilt somewhere around his neck. We heard no sound, except from the earlier casualty. "Did I hear you say something, Sir?" queried Collins.

On another occasion, we had just landed from the sea and were faced with a very difficult climb up some cliffs. Lt. Highland was issuing our attack positions, and, on him inviting any questions, Collins spoke up, "Permission to tie a couple of bricks to my ankles, in case I break into a gallop hauling me A/T rifle up the cliff, Sir ?" Strangely enough, Highland expressed the opinion that making such a stupid request made Collins the laughing stock of the troop!!

It was about this time that I almost gave the show away and, but for a sporting Medical Officer, I would have been posted straight back to Fort George. We had been going through a very hard period of training which included rugby. This was one game I knew little about and had the misfortune to be playing against a team which included Corporal Wheeler, who was an experienced player in Rugby League with Wigan. During one of his many runs, I attempted to tackle and received the perfect hand-off under the chin. I cartwheeled several yards before landing awkwardly on my weak leg. The knee became badly swollen and I feared that if I had to report sick my secret would be out. When I reported for another bout of sport, the next day, I asked to be excused - a highly irregular Army request - and I was left in no doubt about the outcome if I didn't go on a special sick report and produce the required certificate.

I had been concerned about this happening ever since leaving Fort George, but thus far no enquiries appeared to have been made. The Medical Board, however, would have expected me to appear when the Board met and now I was faced with this hurdle and duly appeared at the M.I. Room on a "special." Cpl. Thompson, Medical Officer, on examaining the knee, immediately spotted the cartilage scar and repeated what I already knew. "You shouldn't be here as you are not A1. I am duty bound to report the matter." I pointed out that I had successfully passed in all previous tests and in a matter of two days' rest my leg would be as good as new. In the end, he completed the Certificate,"badly twisted knee, excused strenuous PT for seven days. I was saved again and another two years were to pass before enquiries about my medical category began to reach my unit from the United Kingdom.

We were visited by the then Chief of Combined Operations, Admiral Sir Rodger Keyes, and of course excitement ran high. This was quickly was damped down when he informed us that the "job" for which we had been training had had to be cancelled, meantime, due to other recent events. This was disappointing news but was to be the first of many cancellations. The war situation at this time, December 1949, gave little opportunity to mount raids on enemy coasts while the emphasis was on defence - the protection of our own coast.
The Royal Scotsman had now returned and we again went to sea Most of

our time, however, was spent at anchor, with periods of pottering about in small boats plus odd night landings round the island. Christmas was spent on board but the ship was recalled for other duties and we were again moved ashore, back to our billets. There, then, followed our biggest scheme so far, which proved to be our final test of fitness.

We moved off from HQ and up the Brodick Road for our first objective, Brodick Castle. This successfully completed, we withdrew to Glen Rose, lit some fires and rustled up some food - sausages and mash. Well, in fact, we did the sausages and an elderly lady in a cottage did our tatties to a turn. Needless to say, when Lt. Ravenscroft complimented us on our well done mash, we didn't make him any wiser. Once rested and fed, we moved on up the glen under the usual weather conditions, Scotch Mist, and by the time we had crossed the Saddle and descended down Glen Sannox it was difficult to determine whether we were wet through from the outside or inside.

Darkness came on us while we were yet in the glen, and here I learned never to sup too much water too quickly. Until then we had been denied drinking water and, under cover of darkness, we had soon emptied our water bottles. Lochranza hardly noticed our arrival, although a meal had been arranged for us in the village restaurant. Personally, I was so full of water I coundn't eat. We then retired to a farm steading outside the village and burrowed into the hay and slept the sleep of the fatigued, if not the just.

Early afoot in the morning, and with the help of our small kit, we got rid of hay particles and paraded reasonably well, then found a couple of eggs an, with a sandwich, staved off the pangs of hunger. A truck appeared with breakfast and the great coats which should have been delivered the previous night. We moved off at 9.00am, making for Corrie and Brodick, where we were met by transports which had been sent out to meet us. By unanimous choice, they were sent back with the message that all was well and we were enjoying our outing.

Ne'er day was almost with us and in recognition of Hogmanay, we tried to buy some "Cream of the Barley" and were disappointed to hear that the "local" had instructions to the effect that all purchases had to be comsumed on the premises.
On our way back up to the billets, we called in to see our friend Matthew Kerr and within minutes our supplies for Hogmanay were assured. In addition, we were invited to "First Foot" the Kerrs. Matt was a campaigner from the "Old War", having survived France and Gallipoli, despite the loss of his right arm.
By 7.30pm we, along with hundreds of others, were in, or on the edge of the one and only "local" in the village. Business was brisk, and as time went on it became more crowded than ever and several different groups were singing their own choice songs. Just before 9 o'clock it suddenly dawned on us that whistles were being blown to attract attention and, in the lull, we learned that the bar was dry and that only a choice of soft drinks remained. It was the one and only time I witnessed licensed premises being drunk dry. To add insult to injury, the bar had to remain open on New |Year's Day to meet the terms of the License, though there was not a drop to drink. Davy Gunn, Angus Ross and I moved on to the Kerr's home and we shared a most memorable evening welcoming in New Year, 1941. Singers and entertainers came to light during the evening, and we made many new friends from Lamlash. The most satisfying aspect of our First Foot party was that we were invited back to a Ne'erday Supper, indicating that our behaviour and company passed muster.

By the 3rd of January our "ghost Ship" returned and we boarded once more. We were going on leave for ten days but rumour ws rife. This was strengthened when we were asked to provide railway station details and told that leave was definitely on, and not ten days but twelve. During the last week or two we had had many exercises in full marching order, with full quota of ammunition. In our party, being bombers, we carried fifty rounds .303, 8 primed grenades, as well as large pack, small pack, gas equipment and blanket.

Although we were not to know it, our days in Arran were nearing an end. The Royal Scotsman sailed for Gourock with upwards of a thousand men on board, and I was away to the Highlands once again. My twelve days at home passed quickly enough, and I was not to know that it would be four long years before I'd see Kyle again.

Chapter Eight

We returned to Arran, taking ship from Fairlie and reported for duty. Training was continued where we left off and on the 29th January we boarded the Glengyle, a ship which had been converted to an assault landing ship. All her lifeboats had been replaced by an early design of landing craft and in every other respect, except that we were each issued with hammocks, she was fitted out like a troop carrier. Late on the night of 31st January, we sailed past Holy Island in to the Firth of Clyde and joined a convoy, which included the sister ships Glenroy and Glencairn and a passenger liner with evacuees going to America.

It was a fast convoy, our ships doing a steady 18 knots. Unfortunately, we chose a night which featured a North West gale with driving snow and though some of us remained on deck, the cold soon chased us below and settled us early in our hammocks, before we ran into rough seas off the north coast of Ireland. Reveille sounded while the ship still pounded into a heavy head sea, while the hammocks gently swung to and fro. As soon as our feet touched deck, there was a hurried search for buckets and, in no time at all, one was prepared to share with anyone.

I was a bit disappointed with my performance, having had some previous experience of life at sea but was soon to learn that I was to experience this trouble whenever I returned to sea after a lengthy period on shore. For the next four days, I remained on top of a pile of kitbags and had nothing to eat. But with a change of course and moving south, I decided I would join the boys for supper. The meal featured, of all things roasted hearts (sheep), which arrived at the table in a roasting pan, floating about in a greasy gravy. Needless to say my return to normal feeding was put off for another day.
Our convoy split up during the night and the evacuees' liner, and most of

the escort, continued moving west while we moved troward warmer climes. Our only remaining defence appeared to be a County Class Cruiser and our ships continued to move at some 18 knots. Everyone now appeared to have got their sea legs and normal routine became physical training, lectures etc. while troops shared duties each day. With improving weather conditions, more and more time was spent on deck. After dark, the evening was spent below as we travelled "darkened ship". Reading material was at a premium and, as there were only two or three copies of theWizard and the Adventure, you were lucky if one came to hand.

A total of £35 in cash was shared by some lucky lads on the mess deck and changed hands each night. I had only six pennies in my possession and always seemed to be lucky enough to keep them. I persisted in joining the "school" each evening, but no matter what, my stake remained the same by the end of each session. Some of the lads got a thing about these coins, thinking they brought bad luck. The end came during one of the sessions when Cpl. Donnelly had the bank and, on seeing the re-appearance of these coins, exploded. Before I guessed what was in his mind he had opened the porthole and "Davy Jones" became the proud possessor of six good pennies. Jack was good enough to give me a sixpenny piece but things were never the same again and very soon I joined the ranks of the have-nots. This cash continued to circulate in this fashion until we reached Cape Town. There, the lucky holder at that time decided to send it home to his family while he was ashore and, as we were all very short of the ready by that time, his popularity dropped to zero.

Prior to our departure from Arran, we had been visited by Admiral Keys VC, Chief of Combined Operations, who informed us that we were on our way to carry out a task similar in character to the "Zeebrugge Raid" of the Old War and if successful, would be hailed as the outstanding action of the war. Thus we were constantly attending lectures, and studying plans which were to be re-enacted when we got ashore again. The idea was to mount an assauault on the Italian island of Pantelaria, occupy and hold it until reinforced by the other formations. This island was strongly held and, with underground hangars, it was believed that planes were operating ftrom there against all shipping moving through the Mediterranean.

The voyage continued without incident until making our first landfall, Freetown, where we remained at anchor overnight and got our first sight of the African continent. We were entertained by the divers from the “bum boats” going through their exercise of diving for money and throwing insults at those fly lads who were wrapping pennies in silver paper.

Soon we were on our way and now that the weather was very calm, I moved my hammock up to the boat deck. I remember experiencing a tremendous feeling of well being as we pushed along gently, swinging to the movement of the ship, the moon appearing to swing in unison with the Southern Cross coming in to view and disappearing again as sleep stole over us and all was quiet with the world.On Wednesday morning, 12th February 1941, at 9.00am we crossed the Equator and most of the forenoon was spent in celebrating the “Crossing of the Line”.

On the 14th, we were in the vicinity of St.Helena and on the 19th rounded the Cape of Good Hope, with Table Mountain a sight for sore eyes, the lower slopes the greenest of green. Table Bay, dotted with all types of craft, and the harbour crowded with ships which blew us a welcome as we crept up to our berth. As we moved in, so other transports were heading out, one of them filled with Anzac troops. The unforgettable thrill of listening to “Now is the Hour” emanating from thousands of Maori throats as they moved out to sea, will forever be linked with my memories of Table Bay.

The inhabitants of Cape Town were in tune with their climate, their kindness was legendry and anyone who had the good fortune to pass that way must remember it with with pleasure. We enjoyed their hospitality for two wonderful days, during which I had the pleasure to be taken out to Fischoek and, at midnight, do a spot of night fishing. I had to do some explaining on my arrival back on ship at 0200 hours instead of midnight. I well remember the drive back to Cape Town via the High Road below Table Mountain and overlooking Cape Town, which was fully lit up, in contrast to our own cities so recently left behind. I had received a wonderful invitation to meet a young lady at the dock gates the next day and to be shown the sights of Cape Colony. Disappointingly, we sailed away, heading towards Suez !

Excitement again ran high when, as we were approaching Durban, we learned that the Cruiser Glasgow had detected an enemy raider in the Indian Ocean. She had continued to shadow her, pending the return of our cruiser escort which had left us earlier. As it was not considered wise for our ships to proceed without cover, it was thought likely that we might, after all, put in to Durban until our escort was able to resume duties later. This resulted on one of those on/off situations which had become so familiar in recent months - the ship continued to circle just off the entrance to Durban Harbout, as a series of orders, rapidly followed by cancellations, had us all below decks with one leg in our going-ashore slacks and discarded demins handy for a quick change. In the end the hunters lost touch with their quarry, and as our escort was expected to resume station during the night, our ships continued on course.

Without incident , we sailed inside Madagascar and parallel to the African Coast, reaching Suez on Sunday 9th March and entering the Canal the following day. As we preceeded along the waterway, one was left with the distinct impression that the ships ahead were travelling over sand rather than water. Our voyage ended as we dropped anchor in the Bitter Lake, there to disembark and settle under canvas at Geneifa Camp. It was quite a change after seven weeks at sea and we were anxious to begin final training and polish of the plans for our "Special Task"

The importance of this undertaking became more apparent each day as the latest news from the Eighth Army reached us. It was about this time that we had a visit from General Wavell, then Commanding the Eighth, and during the Inspection we were interrupted by an air raid, which rather spoiled the programme. At that time General Wavell was still enjoying the plaudits of his supporters, arising from his successful campaign against the Italians. The desert sun had not yet cast the shadow of the Swastika over the endless sandsea between Tripoli and Halfaya. Soon we were to know all about the Afrika Korp and share with them, for far too long, that barrren waste which favoured no-one, simply adding to the discomfort of those forced to live there for months on end.

These experiences were all in the future though, and training continued without pause. Now, instead of using models, large scale maps of nteleria were drawn out in the desert sand, including land features, harbour areas and details of buildings and defence positions. The island was strongly defended by air cover - fighters and bombers safely housed in underground hangars - which posed a constant threat to Allied convoys making for Alexandria and the Canal route to the East, as well as those maintaining the link with Malta.

The plan included a block ship which, under command of Admiral Cowan, was to ram the harbour mole, land assault parties, thereafter to be scuttled blocking the harbour entrance, denying its use to other landing craft at other chosen points. The forthcoming operation had, by this time, become almost an obsession for every man involved. Each individual was in possession of the overall plan and was aware of how important his own role was in making the whole effective.

But as the Allies suffered reverses in other areas of the Middle East, our assault was called off, its cancellation received with deep gloom. We'll never know how successful the assault might have been but but one thing is certain - had we succeeded both in the taking of the island and more importantly, the holding of it - many of the gallant ships which kept faith with Malta would have been spared the terrific punishment meted out by enemy aircraft and submarines in the months to come. The situation throughout the Middle East was changing day to day, all to our disadvantage. Germany had invaded Greece and units of the 8th Army were withdrawn and sent there to try to stem the tide. We were not to know that his would prove abortive, and herald one of the lowest points of the war.

The first indication we had of what was to come was the disappearance of our transports from the Bitter Lake, along with news of the evacuation of Greece, resulting in the losses of many of the escort vessels and destroyers which had been intended to cover our landing in Pantelaria. Many of the troops evacuated from Greece were landed in Crete, only to become, in due course, the defenders of that island against Goering's paratroopers. At the same time, it was learned that Rommel's Afrika Korp were making their presence felt to our north and General Wavell was in no position to do much about it as the formations sent to Greece, then committed to Crete and lost, left him powerless.

For us though, life simply went on, with our first visit to the famous city of Cairo, on a short Leave. After a few days there, we were less than impresseed with the local populace which appeared to include hordes of pickpockets, Arabs breathing Garlic and children who defied death on the crowded trams. The Arab boys generally boarded the cars hanging on the outside, with a footing on a slim ridge of wood which ran along the exterior. Usually they were looking for an opportunity to steal and, of course, the newcomers in khaki were like sheep to the shearing.

Due to the climate, windows on the car were generally open and most of the passengers were within easy reach. Once the car had accelerated up to perhaps twenty or thirty miles an hour, the Arab would would step off, facing backwards, with his body maintaining an angle of about 45 degrees. Then, with wonderful control, he would slowly come upright not having moved and inch from where he first made contact with Mother Earth. Meanwhile some poor victim in khaki, a passenger in the car, now far down the street, would be "doing his nut" and breathing fire over the loss of his wristwatch.

On our return to camp, we were immediately dispatched to Port Said and boarded the Glengyle. We were off on another jaunt. On the afternoon of the second day, we upped anchor and proceeded west, keeping the coast in sight. Our objective was the Bardia area. On landing we were to contact No. 7 Commando, who were approaching overland. The objective was to destroy all enemy installations and equipment, and thereafter withdraw overland to base. Glengyle and our escort were to return to Alexandria immediately our landing was completed. But again it wasn't to be. Weather conditions deteriorated during our passage and by the time we arrived off Bardia, with rough seas, bad visibility, as well as heavy surf on the beaches, the landing was called off and we turned for home. Not long after, we heard about the tragic loss of the cruiser HMS Barham, torpedoed in this area with a large loss of life.

On our next return to Port Said, we disembarked and moved to Amyria transit camp near Alexandria. Rumour, at the time, had it that Rommel's para boys were preparing for a drop somewhere in the Mediterranean theatre. Suggested targets were Syria, Vichy French Cyprus, or Crete, even though the latter was defended by some thirty thousand British troops. The 8th Army contacted the Commando Bridgade, asking for volunteers to

Amyria Camp, 1941

reinforce the cover of Cyprus.Colonel Pedder had no hesitation in committing us to the task and in no time we were on our way to Haifa and trans-shipment from there.

This involved a train journey from Alexandira to Qantara, detraining outside Haifa and arriving at the city via many orange groves which were a little less heavily fruited by our passing ! Accommodation was secured on Mount Carmel which gave us a grandstand view of the illuminations derived from a blazing oil bunker, as we witnessed the first bombing of Haifa by the Vichy French Air force.

On Monday 28th April 1941, we boarded a small craft flying the Polish flag and named Warzawa. It had no defences whatsoever, so that during the voyage we were entirely dependent on our own arms. Colonel Pedder addressed us that morning and touched on the serious plight facing our country and Empire, comparing the position with that of 1915 and 1917. He also warned us that, while we had been able to get this ship to take us to Cyprus, there was no promise of one being made available to us in the event of an evacuation. He had volunteered, on our behalf, to Middle East Command fully aware of the risks. At the same time, he made it clear to us all, Officers and Other Ranks, that we were free to opt out if we reported to him immediately after this parade. He said he would arrange for their onward routing to a Reinforcement Depot. Needless to say, there were no takers.

Our sailing was delayed because of enemy activity in the vicinity but we ultimately sailed at 3o'clock, with our Bren guns mounted in the ack-ack position and the Bois anti tank rifle, manned by Collins, ready for anything. An added difficulty was that there were few lifeboats and if the worst happened we were faced with long swim. In fact she was the true "Slow Boat to China" and it could have been one of the passengers on that trip who had the inspiration to compose the song of that title a year or two later. The trip lasted some 19 hours and we landed at Famagusta Harbour without incident and without escort. Just before leaving Haifa news had been received of the Clydebank Blitz and we were sad to lose Cpl

Donnelly, who had been flown home on compassionate grounds.

Cyprus appeared to us like an oasis after our weeks in the desert. No.6 troop was moved to Larnica and camped near the Salt Lake and close to a first class beach. Assault training now became defensive and, in our case, concentrated on the protection of the landing ground and mining of the selected beaches. The overall defence of the island was to prevent landings, either from the sea or the air. We also prepared dumps of stores and

Joe Duffy, Jim Storie and Christie, Cyprus 1941

ammunition in the mountainous Trudos area, in case of being driven from the lower ground, to enable us to continue a guerilla warfare from there.

During this time we ceased to be identified as 11th Scottish Commando but were re-named “Layforce” under command of Brigadier Laycock. Much to my surprise, I was on orders one morning and discovered I had become Lance Corporal. Naturally, I remained in charge of my party, made up of Davy Gunn and Joe Macarthur. News of the German paratroop invasion of Crete reached us and we learned that No.7 and 8 Commandos, whom we had left in Egypt, were on their way to help in the defence of the island. Sadly they only arrived in time to help in the evacuation and were decimated, thus ending any possibility of ever being part of an independent brigade with us. Actually, though we were not to know at the time, this heralded the end of the Commando Brigade which had sailed from Arran in January so full of hope and confidence.

In the meantime, we enjoyed two months of peaceful training on Cyprus. During our leisure time, we made new friends in Larnica, in particular with Sydney Bell and other teachers from the American Academy whose homes became open house to us. Many pleasant evenings are still remembered by those who were lucky enough to be included.

It was on the afternoon of 3rd June, while we were busy on an exercise some distance from camp, that we had an urgent message tro return without delay and arrange to strike and move to Famagusta for further instructions. By 11.00 pm we were resting on our packs on the harbour wall, awaiting the appearance of our ships. It was a beautiful night, which is nothing unusual in Cyprus in June, and we dozed comfortably until about 1.00am. When we were awakened, we found two destroyers, the Hotspur and the Isis, alongside.

There followed the quickest embarkation in our experience and by 1.30 am we were under way and clear of the island, proceeding at 20 knots into a rough sea which at times threatened to wash us overboard. We were all laid out on deck and once the sun came up we were able to pull a blanket over our heads and doze quietly as though we were enjoying a warm bath. The ships made record time to Port Said and on coming into harbour we espied our own ship, Glengyle, at anchor in the roads and, in no time, the transfer to her was complete.

We sailed at 4.00pm and mustered for details of the job planned. The Vichy French had been a thorn in our flesh since the surrender of France, attacking Haifa and off-shore shipping from Syrian airfields. It was decided to invade Syria, with landforces approaching on the coastal road from Palestine and also from the desert. Our job was to make a landing at the Litant river estuary and provide a diversion and enable the attacking troops to lay a pontoon bridge to replace the road bridge which had been destroyed. We had an escort of two destroyers but...on arrival at our intended point of transfer to landing craft we were advised that a recce of our landing points had been carried out and due to heavy surf it was considered inadvisable to make the attempt.

In the circumstances, we turned about and made for Haifa. But hardly had we arrived back when we were told that conditions had improved and the assault was on again for first light. Again we turned about and, with our escort in attendance, returned to the point of transfer, timing our arrival to avoid having ships hanging about any longer than was necessary. Unfortunately, during the recce by the small craft earlier, it had been spotted by the shore defences and, as we heard from prisoners later taken, that the whole of that area had been ranged by French 75s, and sniper positions established.

Minor changes in plans were being made and we now learned that troops 5 and 6 would remain on board, as there were insufficient landing craft available. Suffice it to say, the landing was very difficult and of some 400 officers and men under the command of Colonel Pedder, 44 made the supreme sacrifice, including the Colonel, and some 60 were wounded. Resistance was far in excess of that anticipated and, due to darnkess, objectives were impossile to identify and consequently landings were far too widespread. Some craft fouled the river bar and when the doors were lowered the troops stepped into deep water. Captain (Daddy) |Johnstone of the HLI had a busy time with his walking stick (part of his regular make-up) fishing out lads who were heavily weighted down by grenades and ammo.

Immediately the assault party was disembarked, the Glenelg and her escort were to return to Haifa and as they moved off the group was approached by two destroyers which had appeared from Beirut. While our ships were waiting for some recongnition signal, the Isis received a devastating broadside which knocked her out of action and doused all her lights. Only by the quick laying of a smoke screen by her neighbour was she able to survive. The Glenelg "beat it" on her own. The culprits were two Vichy French Destroyers which had been lying in wait and made such a friendly approach that our ships were taken off guard while they opened fire at point blank range, causing a large number of casualites as well as doing tremendous damage to the Isis.

The Glenelg safely docked in Haifa and remained there for several days until the return of the survivors from Syria (I almost wrote "Victors" but I'm afraid the losses outweighed any successes achieved. The loss of the element of surprise due to the delay in landings, with loss of concentration, defeated the whole enterprise and, of course the strength and grit of the enemy had been very much underestimated. The Australians failed to take advantage of the diversion and the Greys, still with their mounts, were, to say the least, outdated.

It was unfortunate that after months of training and disappointing cancellations, our boys were exposed to such unfavourable odds on this undertaking, their one and only to date. They had, however, proved in the little time at their disposal, that given a less than even break they were the equal of any in the field. Now that only 11 Commando remained, of the original Brigade, and that under strength, we were not surprised to learn that we were returning to Cyprus and would learn of our future role, if any, in a few days.

This time we set up camp in Salamis Wood. It was while there that we were visited by Colonel Laycock, who intimated the demise of 11th Scottish Commando, and who promised us our choice of transfer, if at all possible, to any arm of the service. He proved to be as good as his word.

The danger of invasion of Cyprus had receded and in due course we were relieved by a brigade of the 50th Northumbrian Division, who deserved the rest. The remainder of the time was taken up with taking our leave of our

Cyprus friends and those of the Cyprus Defence Force which had been raised and trained during our stay. Unfortunately, the wives of the English, Irish and French fraternity had been evacuated to Nairobi and they were now lonely men like ourselves and of course the hospitality suffered a serious setback.

The arrival of the destroyers Kimberley and Kandahar, at Famagusta, signalled our departure, for which we were joined by the cruiser Canberra and we arrived without incident at Alexandria. We disembarked and were transported to Amyria Transit Camp to await dispersal. It was sad to break up in this manner after all these months together. The experience of No.6 troop, and no doubt equally that of all the other troops, had been that a partnership had been developed in Sections and Parties where rank and seniority didn't have to be exhibited all time but were accepted quietly and loyally protected by the least of us, which transcended anything experienced in other formations.

The final straw was undoubtedly the cancellation of the “Pantellaria Landings”, plans of which had occupied our full training for months, to a point where we could have recognised any important area of the island without having to set foot on it. The setbacks in the desert, evacuations of Greece and Crete and the cruel losses of cruisers, destroyers and transports, made any prospects of an early return to our original plans impossible.

Chapter Nine

Reluctantly we attended meetings with officers of other units and services and soon our numbers began to thin out, as day after day, parties took their farewells and moved out, many never to meet again. They formed the nucleus of many new units then coming into being : The Chindits, Popski's Private Army. Long Range Desert Group, Stirling's Circus (Later S.A.S.) and 102 Military Mission, i.e. Libyan Arab Force. This latter force were to train for the re-occupation of Cyrenaica, in Libya, when the Religious Leader, Sidi Iariss, again took over.

A party from our troop also joined the 2nd Battalion Camerons at Tobruk, along with our troop Commander, Captain David Blair, unfortunately just in time to be taken prisoner within a month of taking up duties. Captain (Daddy) Johnstone, of the HLI invited some of us to join the Libyans and this resulted in Sergeants Walker, Corcoran and Cpls Fielding and myself moving to a desert camp at Kilo9, overlooking the Delta and there meeting up with the 1st Battalion Libyan Army Force, already under command of Colonel Grant, of the Black Watch and a selection of British Officers, W.O's and N.C.O.s.

A small number of commandos remained at Amyria, under command of Colonel Keyes, in the hope that some task would present itself, in time. These were the men, with some reinforcements, who mounted the "Rommel Raid", with such dire consequences in later months.

Our arrival at Camp Kilo 9 marked the beginning of a long period of desert life, in time becoming real denizens of the "Blue" and developing the characteristics of the "Gerboa" and the "Gazelle". In the early stages, , we were occupied in patrol work and lines of communication, also supplying guides to the Long Range Desert Group. Many of the Arab troops had served in the Italian forces,only partially trained and it was our job to polish them up a bit. It was not part of my plan to become an Orderly Room Sergeant, as I had already experienced such duties in France and this did not appeal. However things were still a bit disorganised and I was prevailed upon to take up the work until such time as a suitable person became available.

During the occuaption of Cyranica, Libya and Tripolitania by the Italians, a Colonial Army, supplemented by local volunteers, had kept the peace. But as soon as the present hostilities had started and the Italians had been pushed out of Cyranica and parts of Libya, the old religious leader, Sayed Idriss, re-appeared from hiding, and with allied help, recruited many of his subjects, from their Italian Masters, to form an independent force to take over control of the country whenever the Italian occupation ended.

Training soon took up our complete attention, although we were urgently required by the 8thArmy to follow up Wavell's attack, which had been renewed on the 15th June. By 21st June little headway had been made; in fact our losses had been substantial and our abortive attempts to save Greece and Crete with the consequent loss of troops and warships was now being felt. Our improved armour was still no match for the enemy and the attack very soon lost its momentum and General Wavell became another casualty. Command of the 8th Army was taken over by General Auchinleck (Auk).

By this time we had moved into positions at Sidi Hanish, just east of Fuka, and covering a Fighter Drome occupied by the Shark Squadron. On the 22nd we heard the news of the German invasion of Russia, which at the time didn;t seem very important to us who had our hands full with the position we were in the desert. In retrospect, it was probably an indirect blessing to us, as the Desert Fox was undoubtedly being neglected at the Germans focussed on the Russian front. The enemy had suffered heavy losses in the recent fighting and, though Rommel was to prove himself a brilliant tactician, he was not yet ready to commit himself to the full. Fortunately for us, the forces defending Tobruk played a tremendous part and our troops, making full use of the all-round defences available, withstood all efforts made to dislodge them. In so doing they prevented the enemy from attempting a full scale attack on Solum and Mersa Matruh and entry.

The result was stalemate and so we continued training, gaining recruits regularly, with more officers and N.C.O's to bring us up to battalion strength. A further battalion was being formed, to meet lines of communication requirements, thus freeing troops required to improve the fighting strength. We were informed that, in the recent fighting, some Senussi Arabs had been taken prisoner by the enemy and, treated as traitors by the Italians, had been executed without exception. Thus, no risks were to be taken in future actions but, rather, we were to move them to the rear rather than expose them to this danger.

Our Camp was situated on the coast and bathing facilities were excellent. It was amusing to find that, with wearing little dress and exposed to sun and sandstorms, it was difficult to distinguish your comrades from the Arabs when you were coming to join them on the beach. We soon discovered that the surf, peculiar to the Mediterranean, could be very dangerous, with a difficult undertow and several of us experienced some anxious moments when we failed to sense the danger. It was only after some of these incidents that we learned that the unit previously camped here had actually lost three lads in this way.

There was much work to do. The orderly room had taken shape and life wasn't too bad, though a bit isolated, and we were fast making friends with the Arabs. The Sheiks were all of officer rank and we began to learn all about life in the desert. On one occasion we were invited to visit an Arab tribal camp and were invited to join them for a meal. Women hardly appeared at all and we squatted in a circle, with a huge bowl or basin full of a mixture like porridge but of wheat containing raisins and chunks of boiled mutton. You picked a piece of mutton and dipped it in this gooey mixture which, in fact, tasted quite palatable. Fortunately, only the senior officer present was expected to accept the more gruesome titbits on offer.

Our companies were taking up additional guard duties at other points and detachment supplies created a demand for additional transport which resulted in our vehicle strength being increased accordingly. I was lucky enough to be sent to Cairo on a course for ten days.

The city was in a fair state of unrest, militant sutdents were parading the streets chanting anti-British slogans and trouble was rife whenever they came into contact with our troops. The situation worsened when a British nurse and an army officer were murdered. Thereafter, any troops coming into the city and falling foul of any student gathering showed little mercy and many of the places of entertainment were smashed up. Things became so bad that all leave to the city was cancelled for a time. Troops employed within the boundaries only appeared on the streets in parties. The crowning insult was the attempt made by King Farouk to do a bunk, intending to flee to Italy seeking sanctuary fromMussolini. His yacht was intercepted and he returned and was confined to his Abdine Palace, while a tank unit of the 7th Armoured Division, which had been withdrawn from the desert, patrolled the streets to prevent any public disorder.

On my return to my unit I discovered that they had moved up to the Mersa Matru area and were now patrolling the Siwa Track, which gave access to the oasis of that name. Reports were coming in that all was not well to our west. Rommel was again outwitting us, striking with uncanny accuracy at the most vulnerable points of our front. Our tank losses over two or three days were catastrophic and large numbers of our troops had been cut off and forced to surrender when their ammunition ran out. The enemy's outflanking methods were forever catching us out and the fame of Rommel had begun to assume the quality generally attributed to, for example, Alexander the Great."

Situation reports were reaching us by the hour, indicating a headlong retreat was in the offing and that many of us were about to experience a repeat of not so long ago. So the various names of desert places between Benghasi and Amirya had almost become as familiar as the railway stations between Inverness and Wick. The 8th Army had become dispirited and, despite our day and night bombing, they were unable to stabilise the front. Later in the evening, the evacuation of Mersa Matru had begun and the light of the fires could be clearly seen from our postions.

We had been strafed wickedly just before dark, though we got away with little damage or casualities, thanks to the prompt assistance from the "Shark Fighter Squadron" who chased the raiders away and brought one down in our area. We were in the midst of a meal, and enjoying some tinned potatoes, beans, peas and "bully" (which in these lean days was considered a treat) when they came at us out of the setting sun. In the ensuing stramash everything went for a burton. It was hilarious, when calm had been restored, to see us all crawling along on hands and knees retrieving as much precious food as possible,blowing or rubbing the sand off it, before putting it back on the plate.

So far we had no orders to move and, though we had scoured a wide area, there was no trace of the 10th Indian Motor Brigade, with whom we were to share patrol duties. Units of the 50th Northumbrian Division had crossed our front during the night but had completely disappeared by daylight. Just after, we heard the rumble of approaching armour and moved out to make contact. Fortunately we approached the staff car at the rear of the column and, with the improving light, managed to identify it and its occupants as German. We immediately opened fire, at the same time beating a hasty retreat toward our own lines.

The exchange had a heathfire effect and firing began all over the place. A New Zealand battery had taken up position behind us during the night and were unaware of our existence. They immediately engaged the enemy tanks and we found ourselves in no-man's land, being showered with shrapnel from shell shortfall. We quickly mustered our transport, which was well camouflaged in a neighbouring wadi, and which gave us a covered exit toward the New Zealand lines, but as soon as they saw us we came under their fire. We continued to move and, fortunately, were identified before any further damage occurred. On reaching their lines , we learned that our unit was to proceed to Fuka and take over defence of the aerodrome.

There was still no trace of the 10th Motor Brigade, nor were any planes to be seen in the area. Obviously both parties had got the message and departed and it was only then that we discovered our most recent orders were ten days old. Meantime, all passing traffic was going in only one direction, to the Delta. We now learned tht one of our companies, on detachment, had not yet shown up and Captain Pollard, our adjutant, volunteered to go back and hopefully get them back into the fold. I had no choice but to accompany him and you can imagine the queer looks we got from all those they passed on their headlong flight to the safety of the Delta. Fortunately, we had only travelled some four miles before meeting our lads on their way to rejoin the battalion.

Previous withdrawals had had some order but here there was disorder. The double width road was so badly overcrowded that many of the vehicles had taken to the desert, just hoping they missed all the dangers of becoming bogged down in the odd areas of soft sand to be found in the most unexpected places. The situation had now become desperate and could only be compared to that of our experiences at Dunkirk. We were also conscious, ohowever, of the fact that if Rommel had had the air support that we had, it would have been far worse. Our planes were constantly giving cover and enemy sorties were now confined to night operations.

At nightfall all movement, which would have been impossible without using lights and inviting attack, ceased. We laagered for the night at Dabba Station and had just settled down alongside our trucks when the first enemy raid was mounted. Several flares floated down over the railway sidings and soon the first bombs were dropping on top of a tanker train, loaded with fuel. In no time, one of the tanks went up and the remainder of the night was spent as far away from the station as possible, where it was as bright as midday.

The withdrawal to Amyria and the Cairo/Alexandria crossroads was rescued at first light but it was then discovered that a new system of defence lines was being prepared. On our arrival at Amyri, we observed that the 9th Australian Division had moved in and were busy preparing reserve positions there. Those of us who were part of this debacle could see little future for any of us unless sterner measures were introduced to stop the rot. Although we were serving with the Libyan Arabs,we had already made up our minds that, as far as we were concerned, there was no more retreating for us. Unofficially it was decided, if Rommel was not held at Alamein, we would join up with the Australians for what could only be the final stand for the 8th Army. The enemy were threatening the Baku oil fields, opening the way through to Persia/Iran and Palestine and the other claw of the pincer. There just was nowhere else to go.It was indeed a black outlook.

Despite our serious position, the Cockney soldier could always be depended upon to lighten our darkness, showing some of the nature of those so valiantly standing up to the Blitz at home. A roadside NAAFI had been abandoned and the stores were on offer, free. The beer was getting big licks and between mouthfulls one lad was heard to say “I must contact my broker and arrange a purchase of some of the Suez Canal shares. They'll be going cheap tonight.!”

For the next few days the situation remained fluid but we began to feel more confident and it became evident that the enemy had advanced too quickly and required some time to re-organise and allow his supporting elements to catch up.I was never able to understand the reasons behind our sudden collapse, but if it was the intention of our High Command to stretch the Afrika Korp, making for an easier landing for the 1st Army in North Africa, they succeeded beyond their wildest dreams. Rommel was now faced with a line of communication extending some two thousand miles and very shortly to be faced by another army.

With the fall of Tobruk, Auchinleck himself had taken over command in the field but it was much to late to save the crippling losses of men and material in the debacle. Many of my colleagues from the 11th Scottish had suffered, either at Tobruk, or with “Stirling's Circus”, on an abortive parachute drop on enemy airfields in the Benghazi and Derna areas. Unfortunately many failed to survive.

Our unit was now directed to the Wadi Natroun area, to begin patrolling the approaches to the Quatara Depression. As we knew, our Long Range Desert Group was capable of negotiating this, when proceeding to their rendezvous at Kuffra Oasis, and there was the danger that the enemy would try as well. Our Beaufighters were very active during the moonless nights and were proving highly successful.It was while searching for an enemy crew, from a bomber which had been brought down the night before, that we came upon a monastery deep in the desert. Needless to say, we didn't have to look any further for the survivors and our Adjutant, Captain Reginald Pollard, of the Devon and Cornwalls, had a field-day using his gift of languages to interview his prisoners..... and the Monks.

The Alamein Line was well established now and large formations of troops were arriving, including the rebuild 51st Highland Division, as well as many improved versions of tanks mobile artillery and 3/7ths and 4/5ths. At this time, Rommel was finding things more difficult. His stretched lines of communication were being constantly attacked from the air and mobile land forces were raiding his supply dumps. But more serious was the onslaught on his tuel tankers and troop transports when crossing from Italy to Tripoli. These only attempted the crossing now in darkness to avoid interception, a sure fate which awaited the air transports to which he had now resorted. By July, Rommel had come to the conclusion that, for the first time, time was on our side and it was now or never for him.

When the 9th Australians took over the Coastal Sector of the line, they, in typical fashion, tested out the enemy formation facing them and advanced some two or three miles, causing a buckle in the front to their left. It was here that Rommel decided to attack. Like a good scrummager, his Korp rolled around the pack, opened up a gap and allowed their armour to pour through. No doubt he fully expected a general withdrawal by us, as was our habit in the past. The Order of the Day, however, was different this time: "Standfast – and close the gap."

For two days the enemy column moved forward with the aim of cutting the Cairo/Alexandria road, some thirty miles away. The opposition met amounted only to light bomber and fighter attacks but, with the lack of air support, the column was sustaining a lot of damage. Now the sheep dog tactics being employed by the Allied armoured formations would tell. Rommel's decision to turn back was the signal for all out assault by our Land and Air forces and resulted in his loss of ninety seven enemy tanks in one day. All this time our troops were continuing their effort to close the gap, but you've got to hand it to Erwin, his column still managed to pass back through the Line. But he had suffered and, in fact, his losses of these two days were never made good. He did, however, accomplish something which didn't seem important then but which we were to learn to our cost, was vital, during our attack in October. While his defensive troops held open the gap for his return, his sappers used the time to lift all our landmines and re-lay them, so that when we mounted our assault, our forces had to pass through an unexpectedly doubled barrier of mine fields - much to our cost.
Now General Alexander arrived to take over the 8th Army Command, along with his field Commander "Straffer Gott". Unfortunately, this latter's plane was shot down while he was on his way to take up the new duties. The tragic loss of this brilliant officer was a blow, and necessitated another appointment, bringing to us General Bernard Montgomery. For many, this was an unpopular appointment but I would say that, for those of us serving

in the desert who had witnessed previous goings-on, the change brought a new spirit to a jaded 8th Army and a partnership which took them from Alamein to Sangro. General Alexander visited our unit shortly after and his reaction on seeing the minefields alongside the Cairo/Alexandria road was anything but favourable. He promptly ordered the mines lifted and sent up to the forward area where he reckoned they could be more usefully employed.

Out of the blue, I received a Field Postcard from my younger brother Jack, who had recently arrived in the "Theatre" and was stationed with his RASC unit somewhere in Palestine, running supplies to the Russians, routed via Iraq and the Caususes. It was now now almost two years since I had seen him, or any other member of my family, so you can imagine my feelings. I began to make enquiries about a spot of leave, and, in the meantime, wrote back suggesting that, if he could arrange for some leave too, we could meet on a given date at the St.David's Hotel in Tel Aviv.

I had been in the desert now for upwards of six months and had amassed a fair balance in my Pay-Book. With the blessing of Col. Smythe and Capt. Pollard, I was on my way to Palestine. I had been in the hotel for three days, without Jack showing up, and was beginning to think he wasn't going to make it. While hanging around the hotel, I had persisted in trying my luck with the fruit machine (it was the first I'd seen) and I had just put in "another nickel" on my way to the main door for one more look, when Jack's appearance, at last, co-incided with a tremendous rattle of coins from the machine. Lo and behold, our spending power was increased by some ten pounds. We had a wonderful week together before we parted.

On my return to my unit, I learned that Capt. Pollard was leaaving to join the Durham Light Infantry, serving with the famous 50th Northumbrian Division. He was a brilliant Officer and outstanding linguist and became Brigade Intelligence Officer with the 50th. Sad to say, he was killed at Mareth some months later when trying to link up with a unit which had been cut off during heavy fighting. One of his last acts before leaving us was to recommend, with the approval of Col. Smythe, that I go forward for a Commission. This was approved by 102 Military Mission and, in due course, I proceeded to No.1 Middle East Officers' Selection Board, Cairo.

This was a preliminary three day course which gave you a series of tests under the observation of a group of officers. At the end, they came together and decided the suitability of each candidate to go forward for the Commission. I enjoyed taking part, although in the end I was not considered. I was of the opinion that the senior officers who had recommended the candidate in the first place, and who had had the advantage of seeing him under all confitions, were in a much better position to judge him that the senior Board Officers, who appeared to be products of the Old School. They seemed to want to hear that a candidate had gone to a Select School and was rolling in the filthy lucre. The fact that Kyle Public School was very select, admitting no more than eighty pupils, cut no ice. All that was required to stay the course was to bluff your way through, but I never was considered a good bluffer. I ended up making my way back to my unit feeling depressed at having such a great send off a few days earlier and that I had let the side down.

Neither the Brigadier nor Col. Smythe were in a mood to accept the Board's findings and insisted on being given a “full report”. This ultimately arrived but was again considered unsatisfactory and they pressed for more details. In the end, I and many others, were asked to return for re-selection. Unknown to us, the Board had become very unpopular with GHQ Middle East, for their high percentage of failures when so many replacement officers were required. The result was that this particular Board was scrapped and replaced, hence the offer to review past failures. I didn't accept the offer to return but was pleased instead to be promoted to Colour Sergeant with the Libyan Arab Forces.

My experience with the Selection Board had rather an unsettling effect on me and I began to yearn for change. I had now served some twelve months with the LAF and the role allotted to them could only be finalised after the enemy had been driven out of Cyreniaca and Libya, enabling them to take over the police duties for these territories. Meantime our patrol duties continued in Wadi Natroun while new formations of troops and material continued the build up. The day of reckoning was fast approaching.

It now seemed a far cry from the hectic days of panic and headlong retreat, which had offered little hope for us all. However, it was that desperate feeling, that permeated down to the least of us, and the changes in command then brought about which transformed the situation. Rommell's recent failure to reach the Delta helped, but most important of all was the order of the day issued by Monty: “No retreat - No surrender”. This was new, this was positive ! It brought new purpose to these bright moonlit nights, amid this silent and endless sand sea, no sooner freed from the heat of the day to become as cold as the ice fields of the Polar regions before the dawn.

Preparations for the attack were now complete, with units of all types in position, covering wide areas, heavily comouflaged to merge with the terrain and hoodwink the enemy reconnaissance planes who, even if they succeeded in penetrating the screen of our patrolling fighters, must have had great difficulty in identifying the true from the false. Even our own ground troops found it difficult to recognise the dummy formations for what they were. It was quite common for a despatch rider to visit a location one day and find it deserted on his next call. On the night of 24th October the long awaited roar of artillary signalled the beginning of the Battle of Alamein, the gun flashes like the lightning spectacular which accompanied a thunder storm we witnessed afloat in the Mediterranean.

Rommel had made full use of the time left to him and the double depth minefields served him well. The task of the sappers to clear a path for the armour was a prodigious one. Several days and nights of probing were to pass before a breakthrough was made on 4th November and the pursuit was on as our armour began to pour through the gap. Rommel had already set his withdrawal in motion and had the good fortune to be aided by the elements - torrential rain in the areas of Baguish, Fuka and Mersamatruh, very effectively slowing down the pursuit. Once again nature had taken a hand to thwart our plans. It was remarkable how often these incidents favoured the enemy in the desert - here we were having rainstorms in an area which we had lived for the past two years without ever seeing a shower of rain.

We soon joined the trek to the west, being informed that our objective would be Benghasi and our Unit would take over control of Libya and Tripolitania, as soon as these areas were cleared and re-occupied by the Allies. This was to take longer than anticipated and Christmas 1942 was spent in Beda Litoria, just west of Derna, comfortablt billetted in empty buildings vacated by the Italians. During of advance to Derna, we were able to pick up, among other things, two pigs which had been abandoned, as well as a fine assortment of fresh vegetables and huge packs of dried vegetables, the latter proving the best fodder available to keep the pigs in good shape for Christmas.

Major Blaber, 2nd i/c, ran a butcher's business in normal times and he contracted to attend to the dressing of the pigs when the time arrived. He required some assistants and I, along with others, volunteered to help. The day came and we were amazed to see how the Major adapted so many bits and pieces to carry out the job. But the fact that his assistants weren't so bright made his task all the more difficult. First of all a small garage had been found to serve as slaughter house and the idea was that, as soon as the animals had been killed, they were to be strung up by the hind legs, to help the bleeding – which promptly sickened some of the assistants. To crown all - literally - the roof beams were unable to take the weight and the roof caved in.

He wasn't going to be beat, however, and somehow managed to get get the carcasses to the stage of shaving off the bristles. Those who were involded will always remember the occasion and no doubt recall the wonderful job he made with his rugged assortment of tools. Once the cutting-up was completed, we brought our share to the sergeants' mess, but on presenting them to the Cook he uttered one word, “Shit.” He, being an Arab, abhorred pork and this had not registered with us. They wouldn't even touch the stuff and so I volunteered to prepare the roasts on Christmas Eve.

Many of the Italian settlers had used a form of Aldershot Oven for baking, which were in fact brick kilns without a chimney. They were very effective... if one knew how to use them. The correct procedure was to build up a fire inside and, immediately sufficient heat had been generated, you swept out all the fire, pushed the roasts inside and and sealed the door. I had never been a cook but I had some idea and firstly spread plenty of butter on the pieces, plied the oven with a roaring fire, then removed the flaming wood, left the red hot ash and slid the roasts in before sealing the door.

It was a bit of a handicap not being able to examine their progress but, from the sound, they were roasting alright, if not already on fire. I couldn't risk it any longer, though, and opening the door found they'd actually gone up in flames. In the end I brought them back to the mess and began slicing up up the roasts and frying the pieces seperately. In the end, all had a good, if unorthodox, Christmas Dinner. In any case, the boys coundn't say very much, as I had spent the last two days back at Tobruk bringing back a fair supply of the “Crater”, to help their digestion.

The troops entered Tripoli on 23rd January, by which time we were settled in Behghazi, occupying the Italian Barracks there. I for one, felt that our job was now complete and raised the matter with Colonel Smythe,of the Border Regt. who was then our commanding officer. I learned from him that he was leaving soon to take up an appointment with the Iraq Levies and was keen that I joined him in his move. I felt I had had enough of the desert life, though, and hoped to take part in the invasion of Sicily which we then being planned.

It was some months before we were free to move and the liberation of

North Africa was not to come about for some four months, despite the successful landings on 8th November. The clearance finally came on 12th May 1943 and I was quickly on my way to Cairo, for clearance from 102 Military Mission. I joined a draft bound for Sicily via Geneifa, where we were held up awaiting orders to proceed to Alexandria for embarkation as soon as a ship became available. Thus I finally shook off the dust of the Western Desert for the last time and the voyage to Syracuse was completed via Malta, with no more incident than meeting the Italian Fleet under escort after their surrender some days before.

Chapter Ten

The Eighth Army had crossed the Messina Straits on the 3rd September and we travelled overland to Catania, moving into a transit camp which we discovered harboured some thousands of troops and refugees of many nationalities. When our party approached the entrance gate, the sentry gave us our space allocation as “six men to a tree”. No doubt many of the draft yearned for the warmth of the deser, as they sat huddled round a tree with only a ground sheet to protect them from the rain, that was to continue for three days. At meal times one had to join a queue which appeared to be a mile long. Our draft was under command of a Major from the Argylls, who had appointed me to look after the food supplied and I in turn had a very able assistant, Chris Rae from Hawick. We were lucky enough to be able to ensure that there was always plenty to spare in case of an emergency and this reserve stood us in good stead while remaining in this camp.

The 51st Highland Division was resting in Sicily and I was given the chance to join them there. However, knowing that they were likely to be returning home, and with the certainty of my then meeting up with that Medical Board, which had been looking for me since September 1940 at Fort George, I decided to join the 8th Argylls instead. This unit was part of the 78th Division, now with the 8th Army under Monty and somewhere between Fogia and Termoli.

Our short sojourn in Sicily gave us the first taste of, once again, being among greenfields - a welcome change from the sand and the cursed flies that were with you all the time. One incident even gave us a real touch of home. We had just erected some tents and no sooner were they up than we were battered by a cyclonic storm of wind and rain. By the time it ended, we were back to square one - not a tent standing, soaked bedding and disconsolate lads who had fought it out but in theend gave it up as a bad job. During the height of the storm, I was directing operations with entrenching tools, in an attempt to bar the water from inside the tents, and happened to look around and observed a couple of lads sitting on an eight hole box latrine. It had lost its decency screen, and they were sheltering under a ground sheet and sharing a cigarette with not an apparent care in the world. They seemed to convey the message, first things first.

Our move to Reggio Calabria also held a surprise for me. It was while lining up the parade for departure that a young airman kept breaking rank in an attempt to speak to me and, though I bawled him out, he persisted. On finally reaching me, he peered into my face and said, “You're Christie, aren't you?” It was Jack Maynard, a lad from home. He had had great difficulty in recognising me behind the moustache which I had grown since we met last. Though Kyle was a very small village, I had many similar surprises during my wandering overseas.

We crossed the Straits by MTB, and resumed our journey to catch up with the units. Fortunately, our arrival was delayed because, but for that, we would have been involved in one of the Argylls most difficult engagements. Commando Units had landed at Termoli and were successful in driving the enemy out of the town. Before withdrawal they had handed over to the Argylls, who continued the advance up the coast. During the night, though, the enemy counter attacked, with the benefit of an observation post left in the tower of the local church and undetected by the Argylls. The O.P. had a clear view of the concentration of troops and the approach roads to the town and brought down heavy artillery fire on these targets.

The counter-attack included a troop of Tiger tanks, and, as the bridge across the Biferno had already been destroyed by the enemy, all our supporting armour was still held up on the wrong side of the river. The forward elements of the Argylls were by-passed during the hours of darkness which enforced a withdrawal by the leading companies. Brigade

HQ which had been set up in an abandoned brickworks, was soon to become the only position held north of the river. The Engineers, struggled manfully to repair the bridge but they were shelled incessantly, suffering a number of casualities, and our 25 pounder artillery support were reported to be firing over open sights. The situation became desperate. All but one of the anti-tank guns had been knocked out and the enemy clearly expected, and requested, the troops now clustered round the brickworks to surrender.

Sandy Forbes, of " I" Section, who was involved in the party, told me later that, with the encirclement completed by Tiger tanks, which continued to pick off targets from the high ground overloking the town, he shared the feeling of many of his compatriots that the door was almost closed. While many thoughts crowded his mind, he suddenly remembered that he had a tin of creamed rice pdding - his favourite dish - tucked away in his pack, which he thereupon fished out and devoured in record time, unable to bear the thought of it falling into the wrong hands.

The engineers, however, had persevered in their efforts to bridge the river and, in the nick of time, managed to get some tanks across. Although the first arrivals over were promptly knocked out, soon they were over in sufficient numbers to fan out and engage the enemy. In addition, the Irish Brigade, who were in reserve, came to the rescue and soon the enemy had resumed his withdrawal to the North. All agreed, though, it had been a close run thing. The end of the action was again marred by the loss of a valuable officer - Major Anderson VC (who had earned his decoration at Longstop) killed by one of the last shells to fall.

Our party of re-inforcements joined up with the unit immediately after their gruelling experience and they were resting in a farm just outside the town. The unit was under the command of Colonel Scott Elliot, of the KOSBs, with Major Hamish Taylor, 2 i/c. On interview, I had to revert to Sergeant and was posted to the Intelligence Section. I had no previous experience in this type of work but was soon to discover this was my real bent and regretted that I hadn't given thought to this type of work before. Being a Seaforth cast among Argylls I didn't expect any kudos and made some acquaintances but not too many friends. I was lucky, however, to have a good section, lads who hailed from different parts of the country and, like myself, were prepared to put up with things as long as hostilities lasted. I was never complimented on my work but on the other hand I was careful to ensure that what I did do couldn't be easily faulted.

Experience in the early days of active service taught me, sometimes at a cost, that you carried out orders first and, later, if you thought they were wrong, let them know about it. With Special Service Units, the emphasis was placed on attack and, far too often, the plans for afterwards were given much less thought. The results more than undid any success gained. It was this training that taught independence and, by the time I joined the Argylls, I had become a unit unto myself and I hope introduced, at least to my Section, a changed form of discipline which served us well during my attachment to the unit.

Corporal Alex MacLeod, KOSB, a ship's broker from Barrow, was my right hand. He had seen service with No.9 Commando and his arrival as a private, to join the Argylls, will always be remembered for this humorous incident. He had a very pronounced accent, more fitting to the commissioned ranks. His transport had been delayed and he arrived at the unit just too late to get a meal. Alex was no less forthcoming than any of his kind who were suffering the pangs of hunger. He approached the cookhouse to find the sergeant resting after his efforts at feeding the company.

Careful to have all badges of rank concealed and in his most polished English, he explained that, due to the delayed transport, his party had missed lunch and was it possible to have anything which might have been left, as he felt raveous. The sergeant fell for the act hook, line and sinker. “Sir, just you make yourself comfortable on this bench here and I'll soon rustle up something for you.” In no time, the meal was ready, some say, fit for a General, and Alex, with the sergeant's utensils, was getting tore in to the good food. He quickly mopped up and then made his one mistake – in a brogue only to be heard in the lowest echelons, asked, "Any buck, Serg?" The silence, I believe, experienced before the onslaught of a cyclone, reigned but for a moment, before the sergeant exploded, "Who the H...are you anyway?" " Private Macleod !" "Get out of here...," followed by many descriptive adjectives, as a hurried departure was made. He survived to spread the tale and the sergeant was never allowed to forget the incident.

I believe his opinion, voiced, to the others of the section, on learning that I was taking over was, "I think he'll be a proper bas...!!" Maybe I was but we all got on well. We only parted when I refused to serve with a unit which, for some unknown reason, condoned an incident in which one of my section was badly mauled by an inebriated sergeant while on convoy duty, but more of this later.

Lance Corporal Sandy Forbes was also a member of the section, a likeable Aberdonian and history scholar who, given half a chance, would expound at length. Early in his service, he had been sent to OCTU and only stayed three days, in his own words, "I coudna pit up wi yon." Sandy could always be depended on when things were rough and he paid the penalty on the Sangro but fortunately hot as badly as we at first thought. The remainder of the section kept changing and were not so esy to get to know.

Our Commanding Officer, Colonel Scott-Elliot, was abune them all, in my opinion he inspired confidence in all those close to him when in action. He used to make life difficult for me whenever I had amended his map, showing the new companay locations and whenever my answers appeared to indicate any doubt he would butt-in "The answer is either yes or no!" I soon overcame that kind of attitude by, first of all, getting Major Malcolm to confirm my map references and then meet the Colonel's query with a challenging "Yes." During my interview with Colonel Elliot, he asked me if I drove a motor vehicle or cycle, and, though I hadn't up to then, I thought there would be little risk in saying that I did drive a motor cycle. His next words put me right in the cart,"That's fine, none of the Section drive and it will be your first duty to train them in the job.!"

I reported to my Section Officer, Mr. Mothereill, who already had been informed of my prowess with the "bike!" and suggested that should be my first concern. He went on to talk about other duties but my mind was solely concerned with getting out of the bungle and my mind was soon made up. I didn't have to prove that I could drive but the rest of the section had to. I called them together and put the important question, "Who can drive a motor cycle?" By the time they had all answered to the effect that all could, after a fashion, it was evident that the only one who couldn't was myself.

I then sent Sandy Forbes to collect the machine and bring it out to a nearby field so that I could see for myself who still required tuition. The field was a bit bumpy but the boys had no difficulty in proving that they were all capable of getting around whenever it was required. I now felt it was most important for me to have a go and try to master this bike. I sent Cpl. MacLeod off with the other members of the Section to give them some map reading practice. They left the bike with me to test it out, before returning it to a lean-to cart shed with open front which was being used to store the machines.

With little difficulty I started the engine, sat astride the saddle with my heel on the gear change and tested the twist grip control. Then I was away, over the bumps.....but also over a pile of rubble that was down in one corner of the field. To say it was out of control was an understatement – all that I was conscious of was hanging onto this "bucking bronco" and getting through the small opening at the bottom of the field. What I hoped to do then was anyone's guess ! I literally flew over the ground toward the shed and, as an eyewitness reported later, bike and rider disappeared into the shed followed by a deathly silence.

Instinct saved the day - as we rapidly approached the rear wall, an involuntary hunching of the body and tightening of the hand-grips caused my heel to come down on the foot brake, stalling the engine at the moment of impact. At the same time, I rose somewhat quickly from the saddle and my head reached out to make a fairly hard contact with the wall. I was still in this position when I heard the rapid approach of those lads who had seen my disapperance into the shed. The first arrival enquired if I was alright, and though I wasn't very sure myself, I had regained control and assured them I was fine. I overheard them in coversation as they walked away, "He must be a cross-country rider." Needless to say I thought so myself and I was to have some awkward moments with this same bike, before getting rid of it for good.

Soon, however, the Section and I became used to each other and I must say remained loyal throughout my term with the battalion. Colour Sergeant Rae was not serving with "R" company and his opposite number C/S. George was with HQ Coy. Both of them had been with me on the same draft and posted to the 8th Argylls. I was, therefore, not without my contacts when extra rations for tea, sugar and tinned milk were in short supply. These items were placed high in the priority list, when moving in to the line.

The junior member of the Section, just recently posted to us, had not yet realised the importance attached to these items, stored in one of our map cases and committed to his care. We were moving up for the Trigno Crossing and I was away early to recce the point of crossing and the area to be covered by the battalion. The remainder of the Section had just put in an appearance and I was looking forward to a good mug of char. The young lad fromYorkshire had the map cases all right but what had happened to the "brew can?" I listened to his explanation with mounting rage and perhaps it was just as well that the real culpret was comfortably ensconced in a quieter corner at base.

Our company CSM had seen the lad carrying the brew can dangling from his web belt and assumed an impression of a mentally disturbed patient. In a frenzy, he had ordered the wee fellow to chuck it away saying he was not to look as if he was a member of a pack of tinkers. The boy was given no alternative but to retrace his steps and find that can "or else"...and, if he was again spotted by our mutual friend, he was told to convey to him my compliments which would be personally delivered when we returned. We had a bit longer to wait for the promised mug of char but never again was our brew can parted from the section.

The same night we crossed the river in darkess and dug-in along the river bank, acting as reserve battalion this time. The attack went in at first light with 38 Brigade supported by tanks and preceded by a barrage of some 500 guns, using 4.05s 3.07s and Bofors with Tracer, which made quite a show. I was dead beat after digging in and liaising with our Company's position. I was curled up snug in my gas cape when the row started and it took me a minute or two to realise what these chains of light were what kept chasing over our heads. This was the first time that I had seen Tracer coming from our lines. Until then, in my experience, it had always come from the other direction. It was a nice change to see the enemy getting a bit of their own medicine

Weather conditons had now become much more like what we were used to on the west coast of Scotland and the ground approaches to San Salvo, our first objective, were very soft indeed. Our armour was soon in difficulties, getting bogged own and becoming sitting targets for the enemy mortars and 88s, that came over in plentiful supply. Despite this, the leading elements of 38 Bde got a foothold in the village and that was the situation when the CO, IO and self moved up to meet the Brigadier and confer at the inevitable Doll's House at the edge of the village. We arrived at the same time as an enemy counter-attack which had now occupied the lost ground and it was a case of every man for himself.

You can believe me that we all felt vulnerable - sticking out like sore thumbs- as we wended our way through blazing tanks and exploding ammunition, to the accompaniment of bursting mortar and artillery shells. Although the CO lost his carrier and unfortunately his (Seaforth) driver, we were surprised to find ourselves back in our own lines unscathed. Fortunately, the reserve elements of 38 Brigade were moved up to add impetus to a renewed attack and, with tank support, re-entered the village left flank. The enemy were soon on the retreat and with the village re-taken and cleared of enemy, the 8th Argylls moved up to join in the advance to the North.

It was decided that the advance would be renewed after dark and our Section made a recce of the terrain to be covered. To assist in locating our start line, I had counted the paces required to cover the distance. The attack went in with our battalion on the right and Inniskillins on our left. I was leading our column and very consciously counting the paces when we ran into fixed line fire, losing one or two men, before being given the order to change direction, which got us out of the murderous line. Concentrating on counting paces as lead hums past your ears is not to be recommended and I wasn't impressed.

About this time, a tremendous battle sounded to our left which went on for some time and Col. Elliot, convinced that the Irish had taken the enemy by surprise and kind of surprised themselves, he quickly consulted hismap and requested a special shoot, by our artillery support, on a road bend just to the north of the battle. The result of the success of that shoot was plain to see when daylight came. The enemy were caught as they pulled out in panic and this, once again, showed the value of quick thinking by a Commander in the field.

Daylight, however, also found us in open country with the enemy holding a high ridge to our front. While we awaited the arrival of our tank support we were subjected to heavy shelling, particularly air bursts, and it was quite fascinating to see the line of troops in front of you ducking their heads in unison like so many puppets. In fact, I think we all continued to duck for days afterwards ! We also learned that, in the fracas the previous night, the Inniskillins had indeed surprised the enemy who in their panic gifted them over twenty 88s which in anybody's language was a gift indeed.

Despite the enemy shelling, we had found reasonable shelter along boundary banks dividing the fields and I had made myself comfortable under the bank of a dried up stream. Although I had been on the go since crossing the Trigno the previous night, I was still standing-by the Brigade field-set. The operators were constantly listening for reports coming from their opposite numbers with the other units in the Brigade. The news of the Inniskillin capture had just been received and I was wandering around trying to locate Colonel Elliot, to bring him up to date on the latest news, but without success.

Our intelligence Officer, Lt. Evans (son of the First War hero, Evans of the Broke) took over to allow me to have a break but when I got to my undercover dugout I found it was already occupied by Col. Elliot, the man I had been looking for during the past hour or so. He was full of apologies and hoped that I could share with someone meantime so that he could get some rest. As he said at the time, "All we require to do at this time is eat, sleep and fight" and I suppose he fully deserved any rest that was going.

The tank supporting the units on our left had already broken through and continued along the high ridge to our front and we were once again on the move. With little resistance, we occupied Vasto, a small coastal town which, we heard had given shelter to many of the Facisti, so that many houses were left unoccupied. We sampled the comfort of a roof over our heads for the night and between us rustled up a satisfying feed while being treated (?) to a dissertation from Sandy Forbes on the reign of Henry 8th and the treatment of his several wives.

We were on the move early before being shaken up by a quick strafe by one of our own Fighters, who didn't expect us to be so far forward, and had us scattering in all directions before realising we were on his side. He

made amends by coming back and giving us a waggle of apology before departure.
Later in the day, we moved into Casalbordino and our Section found a deserted pig sty which, fortunately, was unusually clean and free from the normal aromas that are to be found in these places. With little effort, we had quite a comfortable billet and one of our more adventurous members found a chicken that....must have been hit by a passing vehicle? I had the task of visiting the nearby house and asking the wifie if she could cook for us. I was made very welcome, as I had brought some tinned food, which was a nice change for them and softened the blow of losing a fine laying chicken. Very soon the carcass was sizzling in a shallow earthenware pot in olive oil and being expertly basted as it lay surrounded by red hot ash. This turned out to be another of those memorable banquets, so before moving on we made a further round-up of tins and made sure she was well compensated for the loss.

Now, while delivering the tins, I met the man of the house who produced a bottle of wine which we shared liberally, toasting anyone we could think of. The effects took some time to show ! We were on the move and, as all main roads were under observation by the enemy, we were confined to side roads and mostly tracks. The wet weather had churned up these paths and the mud had to be seen to be believed. It stuck to your boots, both uppers and soles, and it took me a little while to realise that I appeared to be making heavier weather of it than the others around about, having landed in the glaur twice. I was drunk....and the longer we went on the more difficult it became. The R.S.M. Took pity on me thinking I was overloaded. Though he thought it was the number of map cases and picks and shovels that were causing the trouble, he was right in one respect, I was loaded! It took a good number of miles and sweat to clear my brain and I could feel normal again. It had been right good stuff !

We were on our way to Paglietta, a small village overlooking the River Sangro, one of the larger rivers in Italy, and the enemy was well dug in on the north side. All the bridges had been blown and here was an obstacle that was to hold us up for some time. Our section found a building with a large window, obviously in quieter times used by an artist. It gave us an exceptional view of the stretch of river bank allocated to the Battalion and for the next fortnight we manned our OP day and night, pinpointing gun positions and vehicle movement during daylight and gun flashes at night.

It was believed that the river level rose during the night, due to the snow melting throughout the day and only affecting the lower reaches after dark. Constant checks of the water levels confirmed this and we were well aware of this additional hazard, as well as the deep holes and fast flow to be faced when the time for crossing arrived. The escarpment, on the north bank of the river, was so heavly defended by the enemy it was decided that, in the first instance, a night crossing be made. This would involve a rifle company, on a narrow front, with the usual support of heavy MG and mortars.

On the night of the 20th "X" company crossed the river but ran into heavy opposition and were quickly driven back, suffering many casualties. "R" and "Y" Companies crossed the following night and again met with strong opposition. The night ended with "Y" Company back across the river and "R" Company holding a precarious position on the north side. The remainder of the battalion joined them on the 22nd. Much of the preparatory work of the earlier crossings involved "I" Section and our lads had to cross and recross the river many times and guide the others across. In many places one was immersed in the waist high, cold, cold water, flowing fast enough to threaten to sweep the feet from under you. The only way to cross safely was by holding the bayonet scabbard on the man in front and lifting your feet to the minimum required to move forward. By the time all had got across, I, personally, was left with no feeling at all in my legs and when the circulation did begin to return it was pins and needles on a grand scale.

Our section had had a hard time of it leading up to the attack and had little rest or sleep for the previous fortnight. For the first time in my experience, on every occasion there was a hold-up as we moved forward to the shelter of the wood at the foot of the escarpment, I fell asleep standing up and with my head resting on the butt of my upturned rifle. Every time, I came to life as I hit the ground. Despite that, we dug in on reaching our objective and, with my gas cape wrapped around me, I slept like a log.

Our OP was established at first light and contact made with all units on our flanks. Like ourselves, they were to remain in these positions for almost ten days, due to heavy rain, leading to all sorts of difficulties. The weather set-in in earnest and I had an old horse blanket which served best as a roof to my trench while the gas cape served for keeping the cold out and the body heat in. During the night, the blanket had to be frequently wrung out round a convenient tree, to stop the infernal drips that kept hitting you in the face whenever it became overloaded with rainwater. Very often it was a relief to take a turn on the OP.

The original intention was that we held the Bridgehead for two or three days, to allow for the build up of our supporting armour etc. The weather, and the diabolical luck of the enemy, put paid to that as the river rose to flood levels and the bridge erected by the R.E.'s was washed away. As soon as it was replaced, a lone enemy fighter/bomber appeared one afternoon and, unmolested, shattered it with one bomb. It was learned that the 1st British Division had landed recently at Bari and transports, carrying their equipment, had been bombed, while at anchor in the “roads”, along with an ammunition ship which exploded and completed the damage. All this news was great for the morale (!) and the continuing rain and spasmodic shelling made us feel a bit hard done by.

In additon to our normal duties as an intelligence section, we were also responsible for the decoding of the signals reaching us while in the line, many of them relating to changes of divisional plans or affecting other units in our area. Some of them, however, were from army records or some base formation needing information abut personnel who had been away from the unit for some time. I could never understand why they were permitted to reach us in the line when, on many instances, one or other of the sections had to struggle to decode such messages, with the aid of a rifle oil-taper, while sheltering under a groundsheet on their knees in a slit trench.

This did not help matters much as Lt. Evans ordered that all Codex cameras were to be left at base, insisting that it was agin the rules to have them forward where they could reach the wrong hands. We were aware of this but previous experience had taught us it was safer to have them with us. In one instance they were left behind, according to instructions and, Mr. Evans was soon to learn that it wasn't always right to adhere too strictly to the rules when living under conditons were, to say the least, a little unusual. There you kept your head down for only one reason and observed only rules that helped you to survive.

In due course, the inevitable signal came to hand - not only a long message but in one of the more difficult codes. Once he realised the seriousness of the situation, he began to fault me for not insisting on taking the camera with me, despite the fact that I had enlisted Cpl. Macleod to help persuade him to take it with us. Fortunately, he had officially ordered that they be left at base and it was now up to him to take steps to remedy the matter. In the end a camera was collected from base but, to crown it all, the message turned out to be of such low priority it could have been dealt with at base at leisure.......where the required information was to be found anyway.

At long last, weather conditions took a turn for the better and, on the night of the 27th I guided our carrier platoon from the river to our lines and things began to improve. It was now part of my duty to make contact with formations on our right and left and I particularly liked my visit to the Indian Brigade on our left. This generally took place just at daylight when they were busy with little fires making chapatis which, with a ladle of curry added, did me as much good as a large whisky and fairly warmed the cockles of my heart.

On the afternoon of 28th November, a group of tanks from 7th Armour pulled in to our area while we were having a bite of grub and our last brew-up of the day. It was just before dark and a tank commander called across to us asking if we had any tea to spare, as it was now too close to blackout to light a fire. We had some to spare and one of the tank crew came across to collect it. He and |I got on the chaff and I learned he came from Motherwell but on hearing that I came from Kyle, he asked if I was acquainted with Dornie. I just couldn't believe that he really meant Dornie, the tiny village near Kyle, and suggested he probably meant Dornoch. But he was quite sure and told me it had a castle, a picture of which he had in his pack. He was as good as his word and soon returned and produced a picture of Eilean Donan Castle which had been removed from the "Scottish Field" sometime previously. He told me that one of the crew, Paddy, hailed from Dornie, being the local blacksmith.

I hadn't met Paddy before but I knew of him and he came along to see me later on. He was then driving his thirteenth tank, he told me and all the others had been knocked out in action. He had just returned to duty after nine months' stay in Dock recovering from wounds. The very mention of this being his thirteenth tank gave me the tremors and for the next few days he was very much on my mind. The tanks moved in at first light, though not before I had time to slip a quarter mug of good rum to Paddy and wish him well.

38th Brigade passed through us, following the tanks, and it proved hard going for them all. The enemy was strongly entrenched and, for the first time in my experience, were using flame-throwers which made things a lot more difficult. Fortunately, our OP picked them up as soon as they made their appearance and ourArtillery were able to blast them, to good effect. There was little progress all day and, during the early afternoon, Brigadier Howlet, his IO and one other went forward to see for themselves what was happening. While on their way back to our lines, they were spotted and, unfortunately, the Brigadier was killed and one of the others wounded. Our stretcher bearers moved out to bring them in and also were spotted.

For the next half hour we were subjected to some accurate shelling, most of the shells bursting in the trees and causing a number of casualties. Sandy Forbes, on his way down from our OP was wounded with several others and one man died. Lt. Col. Taylor had taken over command of the unit earlier in the day, having succeeded Lt.Col. Scott Elliot who had been promoted Brigadier, to command 17 Brigade of 8th Indian Division. He escaped with a nick above the eye and, when I went in to fill my water bottle at the water-tanker which came to us later in the day, it was beyond use having been pierced by shrapnel.

We moved forward and in support but the following day were withdrawn completely, recrossing the river back to Casalbordino. It was during this withdrawal that I had a chance to get to know our Padre, Capt.Tyson, who had a tremendous way with the lads and I often watched him going about his difficult duties, especially when in the line. On this occasion we marched together and I had started to whistle, which I always did when we were moving in the right direction. He seemed to enjoy it as well and, between times, we talked of far places and what we intended doing when we got home again. My favourite tune, on these occasions, was the "Stein Song" which always lightened up my step. He was a popular Padre and was always to be found with the forward troops, devotedly tending to their needs, even to the end.

On our arrival back at Casalbornino, I was quizzed about the fate of our section motor bike, which I had had to abandon previously when we were at Paglietta. It was there that we again took charge of the bike from our transport section who had had it in their custody ever since leaving Termoli. Brigade HQ was then quite a way to our rear and I used the bike to get there and collect some new maps of the area. The main roads were under observation and daylight travel was restricted to side roads and footpaths. As I mentioned previously, the muddy conditions were impossible on these tracks and before I had gone many miles I got really fed up of having to scrape the wheels which seized up with mud every couple of hundred yards. I was making poor progress.

At one point, I was busy cleaning the wheels for the umpteenth time when I met Capt. Campbell, my company commander, being driven in a jeep, returning to the Unit and I suggested that he uplift the bike while I continued to Brigade on foot. He was a less than helpful type, however, and refused, leaving me to my own devices. I struggled on for another mile or so before the the bike seized up again and, while voicing some unusual adjectives, I spotted an Artillery Sergeant who was quietly sizing me up and shouted, “Do you want a bike?” He smiled and moved down beside me, offering a smoke, and, while we talked, it was agreed that he would look after the bike until such time as we could arrange to collect it. I continued on foot to Brigade and got back to the unit by dark having covered some twenty miles.

For the rest of the time I was with the 8th there were frequent enquiries about the wherebouts of the bike and, up to the time of leaving, we had never made up with the Battery. In any case, it was no loss to our section as it was only made available to us when no-one else required it and underfoot conditions were so poor that the hoof was more acceptable and certainly less trouble.

Our sojourn at Casalbordino was short and the Division moved to a rest area at Campobasso, in the Central Sector, where we remained for a month, enjoying the change of comfortable billets and reasonable feeding. Christmas was fast approaching and we were advised that our next move would occur before New Year, so that we should make the best of it by celebrating Christmas instead. The hunt was on for some of the country's wines and I was able to get a jerry can of vino which proved a bit vinegary. However, with the addition of brown sugar, lemons, oranges, apples and a water bottle of the best rum, we produced a worthy, hot punch in a bucket which was carried around when we first-footed our friends. It proved very popular, with explosive results, half a mug full generally achieving a very keen feeling of well-being, and a second producing singers who sung

loudly and long, until they subsided quietly in the prone position and slept the sleep of the just.
When we arrived at Campobasso, the East Surrey Regiment had been given our billets in error and were settled down and it took some delay before they vacated to allow us in. Some of us took the opportunity to help with their removal and, as winter was now settling-in in earnest, we were able to avail ourselves of some extra blankets. These proved very useful during our stay in the valley of the Sangro, at a point much higher up river from the positions held during the crossings of November. The village of Casoli was our nearest centre, situated high in the hills, overlooking the river. Our companies were spread out and accommodated in outbuildings, the property of small farmers living in the valley.

In the area of HQ Company, there was a confluence of two small rivers joining the Sangro and a very long bridge, standing on some dozen piers, had been constructed to carry the road across, giving access to the farms in the area. The enemy, once they had competed their withdrawal, mined the bridge, blowing up every second pier and when we arived the bridge looked like a switchback. By the time the New Zealand Engineers had finished with it, though, it had become a very low level bridge. They had simply blown-up the remaining piers, giving it a flat appearance and the rubble from the piers gave the water sufficient room to get through.

Our section were lucky to find an empty wine store quite near HQ and, once we had cleaned it out, we soon had a comfortable billet. Since losing Sandy Forbes, we had a replacement to fill the vacancy and he proved to be a very welcome addition to the section. He had been a stone mason in civvy street and, here at Casoli, he proved his worth . In no time at all, he had a hole through the gable wall and, with the help of some iron bars that had come to hand, plus a liberal plastering of that "clayey" mud that was so plentiful, we had a fireplace fit for our needs. To crown it all, he collected some empty tins from the cooks and completed a chimney. We were now having some snow and were grateful for his prowess. The only snag was that, with the introduction of warmth to the building, grape scorpions kept appearing from the many cracks in the walls and were to be found among blankets when tidying up in the mornings. I'm certain they were hoodwinked into thinking it was summer again.

My friend Alex MacLeod was suffering from the cold and could be seen wending his way each morning, complete with balaclava and braces dangling, as he made for a last minute breakfast at the old cookhouse. He had the misfortune to meet the CO on one of his trips and was taken to task for his slovenly appearance. To avoid any such repeats, he made all his visits to the cook house through an almost impenetrable jungle of overgrown shrubs and soon one could detect the beginnings of a path. Unknown to Alex, others had been watching his trail blazing exercise and the end came one morning when, at the entrance to the thicket, a sign had been erected, with an arrow pointing to the cook house and named "MacLeod's By-pass." Alex had to toe the line.

The rifle companies were busy with patrol work and had some successful bouts with the enemy and it was here that, on one such meeting, we encountered enemy troops equipped with the portable-type flame thrower. After the initial shock of meeting this dasterdly type of weapon, they were soon sent back with a flea in their ear.

The outstanding item of interest during our stay here occurred one morning, just after breakfast, when a lad had gone down toward the river with the intention of using up some of that waste paper which he had put in his pocket before leaving the lines. I think he was in the middle of his deliberations when he sensed that he was hearing voices and, though he was certain of his sanity, there was something strange when in open country you could hear voices but see nobody. He quietly moved around and finally realised that they were not speaking English and that the sounds come from a small pile of brushwood nearby. He returned, at the double, and we quickly formed a posse and, in extended formation, surrounded the spot.

As we approached closer, issuing a challenge, a very large Bavarian officer and four other ranks came out with their hands in the air. Explosives and other equipment were retrieved from a trench which had been prepared overnight and cunningly covered over by brushwood. Their mission was to blow up the bridge after dark. Fortunately a lone soldier had, for natural causes, wanted to be alone and had stumbled on the plotters.

The enemy officer was a massive type, wearing an eye-patch to cover an empty socket, an injury suffered on the Eastern Front. I was given the task of taking him back to Brigade in Casoli, taking care always to walk on his blindside. My "David to his Goliath" reminded me of the stories of "Bantams", in the "Old War, when they acted as escorts in similar circumstances.

Chapter Eleven

It was now the middle of February and news began to percolate through that another move was in the offing. Sure enough, we were soon on our way but this turned out to be a switch from the Adriatic to the West Coast, this in preparation for the build-up for Cassino. On the way across, we ran into a severe snow storm and had to seek shelter in the village of Casacalenda, where we were forced to remain for a week. Again our section were lucky to find an underground cellar and, with a thorough clean, fresh straw and the discovery of a fireplace, we were again in clover.

Our stay in Casacalenda served to remind me that I was still a bit of an outcast with the Argylls and seldom did I see our section officer. In fact, we were never sure whether the one we saw last was still with us. For the first time since joining the unit, however, we had an issue of spirits and beer, which made for a change. As it was anticipated that we would soon be back to foot slogging again, it was decided that now was the time to off-load some of the extra blankets we were carrying and any other "baksheesh" that might prove a liability. As it happened, we were advised that our move west was being resumed next morning and our section working party visited the village that night, reporting back later in the evening that their foray had been successful and we now possessed twelve dozen eggs.

Unfortunately, I had waited for their return for so long that I had drunk all their beer and my spirits, but, like the good lads they were, no-one grumbled. We all set-too and enjoyed six fried eggs each for supper and thern found a very large pot and boiled the remaining eight dozen, to sustain us on our journey.

“I” section were never allocated a truck and were always split up travelling on whatever vehicle could take us. It was still snowing when we, carrying all our accroutrements, appeared out of the snow on the village square where the CSM was doing his nut and shouting threats and abuse about “I” section being always late on parade. Of course, I was well aware that the issue watch which was on charge to “I” section quietly reposed in his pocket, ever since my predecessor had been unfortunately wounded in action. He went on to threaten that I would have to appear before the Company Commander, as soon as we reached our destination. I agreed that he was entitled to do that and it would be an opportunity for me to find out the whereabouts of the Section Watch ! This had been missing when I took over the section and it was high time we had something that would give us the right time and, of course, make his life easier.

No more exchanges took place until later in the day when the convoy rested at the roadside for a meal. He came along the column, called me aside, informing me that he realised my difficulties and would forget all about it. I knew I had him on the run and insisted on seeing the Company Commander to have the matter of the missing watch sorted out for good.In the end, I didn't pursue the matter any further. I had a good enough watch of my own, as as long as I knew where the Section watch was, I was content to leave it there - one never could tell when such defences might be required again.

Our section had recently been strengthened by a new arrival, Jeffries, from Dundee and a very much later call-up. He was much older than the rest of us, certainly over 40, and it seemed a pity, at this stage of the war, to find him uprooted from his family and pitchforked into this kind of life. He was a quiet inoffensive, individual and to be honest just like a fish out of water. Naturally, he was the dogsbody, partiuclarly to a sergeant who had arrived with the same draft. Obviously the latter knew all the ropes and it was surprising that, being a regular soldier, he hadn't been pushed out from the home base much earlier. No doubt, the reasons would come to light in due course, but he had already found a cushy job with the unit as Post Sergeant. The poor corporal, a much older man, who had been doing the job well enough, had been returned to ordinary duties.

The convoy had pulled up for the night and were laagering at the roadside. The new sergeant had been detailed to take charge of the piquet. When he appeared at the tailboard of the truck carrying some of my section, he detailed Jeffries for the duty. Jeffries gathered up his equipment and at the same time suggested to the sergeant, "My name is too well known about here." As he jumped down from the truck, the sergeant hit him a severe blow, breaking his dentures and lacerating his mouth very badly.

I was informed of what happened and immediately went to look for the sergeant and challenged him. I was immediately accosted by the CSM who appeared from behind a truck. When I asked that the sergeant be put under arrest, the CSM reminded me that I couldn't make such a demand. I countered, saying I was aware that I couldn't, but he could. He then played his Ace, "Where are your witnesses?" I told him I would soon get them. I returned to the vehicle and I'm ashamed to relate that, now that the gloves were off, not one lad on that truck was prepared to be a witness. The only thing I was certain about was that the sergeant was drunk and was being shielded by the CSM who had already threatened the lads in the truck. There was nothing more I could do, other than making a request for an interview with the Company Commander at the first opportunity.

I was always conscious of a Senior NCO's responsibilities to the men under his control and, in this instance, I could only make an unsupported report to my Company Commander. On our arrival at Capua, now free of snow but floundering in mud, I had my interview with the CC. But it served little purpose and I had heard that Jeffries was being admitted to hospital as soon as could be arranged. On hearing this, I took no further action, as I was aware that when a soldier was admitted to hospital with injuries sustained while out of action, an immediate enquiry must be convened to determine the causes in the event of later claims for pension. As it turned out, someone must have become aware of this fact and the result was that, to my knowledge, Jeffries was never admitted to hospital and was held at the unit sick bay to be treated there. Jeffries never re-appeared, while I served the last few weeks in the Section.

The weather improved and we were now issued with bivvy tents and, as usual, they were in short supply for "I" section. It was to be one tent between two men and anyone who has not had to live in these things, in wet weather and muddy boots, hasn't missed anything. I had recently discovered that an old friend of mine from desert days, Tommy Jones, CQMS, was now with the West Kents and only a mile down the road. A short visit to Tommy and I had a nice bivvy tent for myself which made the visit very worthwhile.

I still felt very bad about Jeffries' injuries and I requested an interview with the Adjutant. At the same time, I had been writing home and, in my letters, I described the unit as the worst I had come across during the whole war. I handed the letter to Mr.Murray, the Censor Officer for that week, but it appeared that, after reading the contents of my letter, he proceeded to show it to the CO. The first indication I had that our IC had returned to the unit was his sudden apprearance at my tent to tell me that he had just been sent up to give me a bloody good bollocking for writing such a letter and making such scathing comments about the unit.

My immediate reaction was to ask him how he, or the CO, had learned what was contained in my private mail. I explained that I had passed it to Mr.Murray, who was duty bound to secrecy on any private correspondence given to him, and if any of the contents were considered a breach of security to delete same. On no account, however, was he permitted to bring the contents to the notice of any other person. I said that when my private mail became a subject for discussion over the Mess Table, it was time that the Welfare Officer took a hand. I made contact with my friend the Padre and left him to deal with the matter. The following morning I was granted an interview with the Adjutant and requested a transfer to Movement and Transport, Royal Engineers, who were seeking volunteers.

A couple of days later we moved up the road to "Million Dollar Ridge", overlooking the Liri Valley and facing Monastry Hill. The ridge was a conical shaped hill which, it was believed, cost the Americans that much to take, hence the name. Our Brigade was in reserve and we spent a miserable time on a bare slope, in muddy conditions and quite near an American gun emplacement. This harboured a 9.2 seige gun, which fired at odd times during the night. Every time it went off, the vibration lifted you about a foot off the ground and if you had a paraffin lantern, you always had to fish the wick up out of the oil. I was talking to the Top/Sgt one day and he described the use made of the gun to remove bridges, in a Southern drawl, "We land one at each end of a bridge and the whole cabush automatically collapses."

I had been on the lookout for a more favourable campsite and, though most of the hills in the area were nothing more than large mounds of volcanic ash from earlier eruptions, I was lucky enough to find one with a rock seam which offered a good sheltered position on a stone platform. Using my tent as a lean-to, I soon had a comfortable shelter, free from all the mud and above all, providing a position where I could build a small fireplace, hidden from observation and thus be the only person able to have a fine hot mug of tea after dark

It was while preparing my supper a couple of days later that I first came across Lofty Foster of HQ Coy. He was on the scrounge for "any tea to spare" and undertook to provide a tasty sandwich in return. He duly showed up with a double slice of bread, laced with lovely fried kidney, the taste of which is still with me whenever I think about it. I was at a loss to understand how he had acquired this tasty bite and I sat back and listened to a man whom circumstance taught never to miss an opportunity to help others while at the same time looking our for himself.

Earlier that day he had been knocking around with little to do and, spotting the Quartermaster's truck as it was on the point of leaving to collect provisions from the the Divisional supplies Depot, promptly volunteered to join and help the working party. On arrival at DID, they were just receiving a large consignment of frozen carcasses, including New Zealand lamb. In no time, he was helping the staff there to carry them in while, with his pocket knife, he was busy severing the kidneys from each. He returned to the unit with pockets full. He was, like all Londoners, hard to beat and was also able to improve my stock of cigarettes, which were in short supply at the time. Apparently, his helping hands always knew where extras could be found.

Lofty had been serving with the Gordons and was stationed up in Yorkshire when London was being severely bombed. He had a young family living in one of those areas being badly treated but was unable to persuade his Commanding Officer to give him time off to checkup on them and, if possible, have them moved to safer ground. He was then a full Corporal and, unable to delay any longer, he “took a powder” and went AWOL. This was serious enough for an NCO but I was shocked to hear that he remained absent for nine months. He gave himself up to the Military Police at Euston Station when he was satisfied that his family were now fairly safe from the bombings while his “Old Dutch” now had a bit of money for any emergency.

He told me that when he first arrived in London, he fell in with an old pal who was still free to operate in the city. I believe he was a window cleaner, but, due to the tremendous damage being suffered by the city's buildings, he decided that salvage recovered from these places offered a new source of income. There was a ready market for bathroom fittings etc, and he persuaded Lofty to become a partner. They were doing so well it became part of the drill that, as soon as the alarm sounded and the sound of the first bombs determined the target, they were on their way across the city. While most other people were confined to the underground shelter, they were loading their barrow, with the job completed before the all clear sounded. It was amazing to hear that night after night they took their lives in their hands to make a bit of money.

You have to hand it to him, however, that, when his priorities were completed, he was ready to face the music and whatever punishment was meted out to him. He was arrested, court marshalled, stripped and given field punishment. He had immediately volunteered for overseas service, which is how he came to join me on that bleak and dark night on “Million Dollar Ridge”, more than comfortable with a kidney wedge and a cigarette.

Preparations for the attack on Cassino were well advanced and the 2nd New Zealand were to make Cassino Station their first objective. Meanwhile an Indian Division were to attack “Monastery Hill” with the 78th Division in reserve, to take up the pursuit whenever a breakthrough occurred. On the morning of 28th February, at first light, heavy bombers began a massive assault on the twin objectives and flights of some fifty bombers continued to follow each other in all morning. The high ground and the valley remained shrouded in dust and smoke for the remainder of the day. The CO arranged for a little celebration that night and we were all treated to a ceilidh and a good supply of hot grog.

It was just coming up to Zero hour when the heavens opened and down came the rain which continued all night, causing no end of trouble to the attacking troops and, worst of all, again bogging down our armour. The enemy used the piles of rubble in Cassino, the result of the bombing, as anti-tank traps, and those that did make it through them were picked off with ease. Once again circumstances favoured the enemy, and in addition to the failure of our spearhead troops to complete the taking of Cassino Station and area, the assault by the Indian Division on Monastry Hill fared even worse. Daylight found the forward troops on the wrong feature and subjected to withering fire from the enemy occupying the higher ground. The situation was almost impossible and we were now advised that the 8th

Argylls were on a twelve hour standby. "The assault on "Monastery Hill" will be carried out by us under the cover of darkness dress, skeleton order and plimsolls." Fortunately for us, the weather worsened and the whole debacle was called off. It was some three months before the final breakthrough was accomplished.

Three days later, I was called to the Orderly Room to hear from the Adjutant the result of my application for transfer to the Royal Engineers, Movement and Trnsport. I was informed that applicants had to be of a medical category lower that A1 to be accepted for this work. As I have already mentioned, I had been downgraded to category B1 in 1940, but I had never appeared before a Medical Board for it to be confirmed. I surprised the Adjutant with this information and he promptly ordered me to go on a special sick report and have this confirmed by the Unit Medical Officer. He agreed that I qualified for the transfer. Obviously this information was passed to the Army HQ at Caserta and within three days a lengthy signal arrived with instructions for my immediate posting to Infantry Base Depot and requesting information about why I had been serving with a First Line Regiment for so long.

On the afternoon of the same day, I handed over the Section bumph and took leave of my lads, sadly, as they had been good comprades and I had never, at any time, had to use rank to get on with the job. I had made other friends throughout the Companies. Chris Rae, of B2 Company and Donald Campbell of Caol Ila, Cook and other Islay boys. I also left Lofty behind but was in no doubt that he would survive and always remain a move ahead. I reported to the Infantry Base Depot that evening and once again I was on the loose.

I hate having to put up with incidents like that of the treatment meted out to poor Jeffries and this move was all that was left to me to show how I felt about the matter. I never intended to put in my Army Service as a "base wallah" at some depot or other. It was with regret that I gave up being Intelligence Sergeant, as I enjoyed the work and the collecting and purveying of information made one feel a real part of the organisation, as well as keeping one abreast of the latest happenings as they occurred. Some three days after my arrival at base, I wass despatched to a hospital at Casera, there to be examined by an orthopoedic surgeon who confirmed the earlier category but, in this instance, recommended further downgrading to B5. On my return, I was informed of the recommendation that I would have to be examined by a Medical Board and, similar to my experience at Fort George, it would be convened in a month's time. I learned from two old friends of mine, who were also waiting posting, that the only duties given to men in our position was guarding men who had gone absent from their units. They were incarcerated in a barbed wire compound in the middle of the camp and they also had to be guarded when these prisoners were being used as working parties, outwith the camp. I'm afraid I had little time for these fellows and it was never my intention to spend my service life looking after these guys. I was in the same position I had been at Fort George, back in 1940, and my mind was made up to move as soon as possible.

That afternoon, an incident involving these prisoners confirmed my feelings, that the sooner I was on the move the better. The Guard Commmander, on duty that afternoon, was faced with a breakout from the compound. They were drunk, having been supplied by some of the local Italians. Two of the prisoners broke out and attacked the Sentry with a broken bottle, which left him with severe infuries to his face and possible loss of sight in one eye. The Guard Commander appeared and, seeing the culprits making good their escape across the field, called to them to return. Paddy was an old hand and he had been told that the last time a similar break had occurred the Guard Commander had been demoted as a result.

Paddy wasn't prepared to allow this to happen to him and if he was going to be stripped it would be for something worthwhile. After repeated orders to return and before the escapers finally disappeared over a railway bank, Paddy fired and brought down the leading man, having wounded him in the leg. The other quickly returned, as the camp stretcher bearers collected his mate who was now to be conveyed to hospital along with his unfortunate victim. You may be sure he got little sympathy from the lads who had witnessed the whole affair. I didn't escape this duty though and, the following day, was put in charge of a working party. Before moving out, I purposefully loaded the magazine, putting one in the breach to make sure that there would be no misunderstandings. Paddy had, of course, been arrested and was awaiting Court Martial when I made my departure and I was never able to learn the result.

It was during my stay here that I was called for interview, with several other senior NCO's to take charge of the C in C's armoured train. This was something new, yet it was typical of me not to be interested. On hearing of the duties involved, I asked to be removed from the list. I was recalled twice by the panel, who appeared to favour me for the job, before I made them believe I didn't want it. Some days later I noticed that the day's detail baord included a notice asking for volunteers for a DISRS Draft - I still don't know what the letters stood for - but I called at the office and had my name included on the list.

The following morning a truck load of us left on this draft and, later in the day, we arrived at a point some three miles south of Salerno, on the coast and sporting a very expansive sandy beach. Tents were already on the site and parties of Royal Engineers were busy excavating building sites and laying tracks.We learned that this was to be the site of a "super rest camp" to provide proper holiday facilities for the troops. Hutted accommodation was shooting up all over the place and I had already been appoiinted to take charge of the administration staff, whose numbers were increasing each week. Within a month we were handling 3,500 officers and other ranks, who generally spent a week's leave, ultimately increasing to 2 weeks. I had now been promoted to Staff Sergeant, which included an additional clerical allowance.

This rest centre soon provided all the facilities required, ENSA Concert parties being attached, for periods covering several weeks, appropriate

Messes providing spirits and beer, and special feeding provided under the auspices of the nearby army school of cookery. This gave the lads a reasonable break, the first for many since leaving the United Kingdom. The appointment of a Sports Officer brought much needed recreation. Class football matches were arranged, cricket competitions etc and of course the swimming facilities were first class. Many football celebrities came to the surface here – Andy Beattie (Preston), Arthur Geldard (Everton), Meek (Sheffield United) and many others. I was fortunate to be included in the camp team and had my moments among some of those stars. It added enjoyment to the game to find oneself sometimes up against one or other of these more illustrious names.

As hostilities moved further and further north, many of our lads, who had been taken prisoner during the Middle East, Sicily and Southern Italy battles, were released from Prison Camps. As these areas were over-run ,many of them found their way to our advanced troops, ultimately reaching our camp for vetting and preparation for onward routing to the U.K.

The outstanding incident, however, was the arrival of 1,200 Russian Prisoners-of-War who had been either in the prison camps or evadees n Switzerland, and Allied Headquarters passed them to us for processing. We were advised that several interpreters would arrive with the party and each soldier would be treated in the same way as our own P.O.W.s. This entailed completing the same questionnaire, despite the fact that none of them spoke English. The idea was that the interpreters would translate as the answers came up. To add to our difficulties, only one interpreter showed up on arrival.

We were already prepared with four reception points and of course, that had to be reduced to one position. Our new Pay Corps CSM had taken over and I took a back seat, to be honest, hoping for things to be difficult. I needn't have bothered, the whole system collapsed;. It appeared that the Russian soldier had no army number, and no English and to process them one at a time was going to take weeks. Once the chaos had had a chance to develop, I went down to see if I could help.

I had a word with the interpreter and, taking one of the questionnaires, suggested he should print in Russian the equivalent of each question asked. This he did and I returned to the Orderly Room and, with the help of a wax and stylo pen, prepared a Russian questionnaire, ran off a number of copies and amazed the interpreter who found them quite clear. The result was that each soldier was handed the form for completion and return. In a matter of two days, we vetted these heathens and forwarded some twenty five copies to the War Office, Allied HQ Russian Legation and anyone else who thought they should be given a copy. A similar party of Russian PoWs had been sent to Bari Rest Camp and they experience many more difficulties. Allied HQ were so impressed with our efforts they sent an Officer to see us and we promptly gave a copy of the questionnaire to him.

We managed to deal with a further party of Russians on the same basis but these nomads gave us more trouble than Gerry. They were a law unto themselves and, in no time at all, they had gone through the Leave Officers lines, pinched anything worthwhile and broken into the Wing Cook-house and stores. They were worse than a swarm of locusts in a corn field. They were allowed to leave the camp and visit Salerno and the poor “Ay-ties” didn't know what had hit them. Our camp police and the town CMP never had a moment's peace. When we insisted on them appointing their own Police Patrol, it's member were the first to appear back in camp under the escort of our own police.

Feelings in the camp ran high and sooner or later there was going to be a real bust up. Sure enough, on one particular day as the NAAFI rations were being issued, the Russians were getting their's issued as well. The camp NAAFI building was very like an aircraft hangar, complete with the usual sliding doors. Unknown to the authorities, a plan of action had been drawn up by the camp staff and the Russians, as they arrived, were directed into the canteen. When it was felt they were all in, the big doors were closed..... and the party got underway. A witness reported that, from the outside, all

one could see was that, every so often, the big door opened slightly and another Russian body would hurtle out.
I had a good laugh when our Orderly Room Runner came on duty sporting a gem of a keeker. As he was anything but aggressive, it was difficult to understand what had happened to him. He told us he had been sitting by himself, enjoying a pint, when one of the British troops just let him have it. A Glaswegian, he looked up at his assailant from his prone position in the corner and asked, "Whit the hell was that fur?" "Sorry Jock, I 'fot you was a Russian," came the reply. We were glad to see them away.

The biggest joke of all was that, long after my own departure to "Old Blighty", large parcels of stationary arrived at the Orderly Room. Guess what? Thousands of questionnaires in Russian ! Far too late for the war – but who knows, in plenty of time for the next one.......

Our advancing troops were now nearing Northern Italy and it was only a matter of weeks before the enemy would be driven out of Italy completely. Plans for establishing a similar rest camp in the Rimini area were well advanced and our experienced staff were to fill the key positions, while further reinforcements were arriving to supplement both teams. As I was likely to qualify soon for posting to the UK. I was to remain with the rear party.

Sure enough, on Christmas Day 1944 my posting orders arrived and, with such short notice, there was little time to make any celebration arrangements. However our friends at the Army School of Cookery took over and provided a tremendous supply of eats and, with a liberal supply of beverages, we had a night to remember and a Boxing Day Morning to forget! Inevitably, brought into use were lashings of OK Sauce and I had to have another bath before reporting for my departure medical.

I proceeded to Salerno Transit Camp, for onward routing, and immediately fell in with several of my old comrades who had originally arrived in the Middle East with me in 1941. With Eddie Ellison, from Stirling, Dougie

Pomford, from Liverpool and two friends from the 8th Argylls, Sgts Hay and Greer, I formed a small unit of our own and enjoyed our trip. I became duty CMS for our Mess/Deck and soon discovered, from the number of men reporting sick, that the ship was riddled with bugs, no doubt picked up during her previous trip carrying evacuees from a Black Sea Port.

Naturally, the officer in charge refused to accept this and maintained the men had brought them aboard. We escaped this menace by opting to sleep on deck using our own blankets. This worked all right until we were well through the Bay of Biscay and came awake, freezing cold and in the middle of a blizzard. Our arrival at the Tail of the Bank showed our first glimpses of home nestling under a foot of snow. By time we got ashore, it was Saturday afternoon and anyone going as far north as Inverness had to spend the time in the Deaf and Dumb Institute – a very appropriate place, my friends said.

Chapter Twelve

Having served the requisite four years Overseas, I was due for a Home Posting and, on arrival in the Clyde, my instruction was to proceed to the Argyll's depot in Ayrshire. From there I was ordered north, to join the Orkney and Shetland Defences HQ at Stromness. On arrival, I discovered what seemed to me to be more troops than were left in the theatres of action. It took me some two months to learn that service in Stromness was considered to be "Overseas", and I realised then why there were so many serving in the Northern Isles. This posting was to increase my Overseas service to four and a half years.

There was another bit of information which I gained while serving in Orkney. This was that, except for tea and sugar, there was little else rationed. Of course, I had to make the best of it when going on leave. This resulted in leaving all equipment behind and using up all my baggage allowance with local produce. You may be sure my arrival home was most welcome. The flight was perfect and instead of the journey lasting some twenty three hours I was home in four hours – quite an improvement.

The quiet life continued until the night of 14th August 1945. We were early in bed and, suddenly, just on midnight, a voice was heard nearby calling out, "It's all over ! " There was a stunned silence, but only for a moment. Then bodies erupted, beds emptied and in a flash all were dressed and making for the Mess. Need I say, there were no absentees, glasses were filled, toasts drunk, and then all was quiet to listen to the news. The party lasted for about an hour and we then, in a body, set out for the town and if anyone there was still asleep, thunder flashes did the rest. The festivities continued throughout the next day and a party of us left for a trip to visit the Churchill Causeway and the Chapel built by the Italian prisoners of war, on South Ronaldsay. We also inspected a German submarine that was on show in Kirkwall Harbour.

Our party returned in time to see the completion of bonfire preparations and witness the final act of placing a wooden barrel of tar on top. Unfortunately, in attempting to roll the barrel into place, it somehow got out of hand, careered down the slope, and, in bumping down a flight of stone steps leading to the lower road, burst open, resulting in a sea of tar covering the road surface and, via a grating, the foreshore. Some of the Senior Officers had witnessed the debacle and sent the Sergeant/Major to investigate. He, like the others, was getting “a bit tired” and slipped on the tarred steps, ending up prone on the well covered road surface; all that was missing were the feathers.

Under these conditions, you are seldom without a bright spark! He decided the only way to clear the road and quieten the irate motorists who had inadvertently had an underseal, whether they wanted one or not, had returned with a bundle of newspapers, spread them out on the road and set them alight. In no time we had a road surface on fire, with flames disappearing down the grating and flowing down the beach as far as the tide permitted. This was witnessed by all the residents of the camp and at least half the population of Stromness. Meantime, the Sergeant Major was ceremoniously carried up to the showers, laid bare and committed to the bath under the eyes of his admiring underlings.

Fortunately, the accident to the barrel of tar determined the bonfire site and, had they been successful with the original plan, there is little doubt that many of us may have been searching for other accommodation. Once things settled down, we all returned to the mess and a good time was had by all. The Commanding Officer had to deal with some correspondence from the civil authorities and we later learned that they got a very conciliatory reply, with the additional remark that he thought the men extremely fortunate.

The month of September was mostly filled by clearing up and noting the gathering volume of information and instructions for demobilisation. Now was the time to reflect on the happenings of the past six years and the changes which these experiences had effected in our own make-up. I felt, and no doubt looked, that much older, and, some would say, was somewhat wiser. It was never my intention to spend my effort tucked away in some office, especially like the one I left behind. Nor at any local depot which, I soon discovered, harboured all the "irregular regulars" and wide boys. Being naturally left-handed, I was immediately at a disadvantage, serving in an infantry battalion. An added handicap was that you were serving with neighbours who were well aware of your capabilities, yet you never had a chance to try something different.

For most of the war, I determined my own service, mistakenly believing that, being absent (under treatment in hospital in Boulogne, then evacuated by hospital ship) when our unit was overrun by the enemy in France, I had somehow let the side down. Don't get me wrong, however, I had no illusions about being a brave warrior. The fact is that I was more afraid of running away than facing the enemy. I believe that being one of a large family, fairly strictly brought up, bred in us a greater fear of ordinary bad behaviour than facing the dangers of war. In any case, these were recognised as being outwith our control and, in fact, when such occasions arose, were accepted quietly, no doubt with body and soul already committed to higher care. These were the occasions when one was again reminded that atheism doesn't exist in a slit trench.

Those who were serving abroad for any length of time, or were, unfortunately, confined to a POW Camp, were, confronted, when released, with many changes in their homeland. The recent election had dispensed with the National Government and had resulted in a landslide victory for a Labour Government which, to many of us, boded ill for the future of this land.- a view which was to be confirmed over several later years. The day of release duly arrived in October 1945 and many of us took our leave from Orkney. We proceeded to Edinburgh and joined the trek leaving Glencorse Barracks, with our cardboard boxes, before taking the train for Kyle and civvy street.

The reader, thus far, might form the opinion that I had enjoyed a pretty comfortable war but, like most returning warriors, I tend to remember the good times and gloss over the not so pleasant incidents. Many of these, if recalled, would inevitably throw shadows on families whose menfolk are really better forgotten. Sadly, some men of good family, whose forebears served their country with distinction and were much decorated for their exploits, felt very conscious of what, they thought, would be expected of them. In striving to emulate their fathers, they took risks which ended in failure and death for themselves and those they took with them. Tragedies were numerous and the price paid was heavy.

When discussing incidents with survivors, one realises how uncertain life really is and how the committance to the Most High banishes fear. Afterwards, one is thankful for deliverance, while remembering the good points of comrades who have missed out, and who you might have been called upon to commit to the good earth. On many occasions, one hoped to "stop one" - as long as it wasn't too bad and only promised a short stay in hospital and relief from a rain soaked slit trench or an exposed ridge, depending on the theatre.

One was amongst a "motley crew", either serving as a regular, volunteer or conscript, all to be welded together to become a unit. Officers' Selection Boards were found in all theatres, drawing from various units, to provide a steady stream of suitable candidates to replace losses in front line units. Their failures, however, became so numerous that the powers that be were eventaully compelled to delegate the power, allowing field commanders to make good their own vacancies from within their own units.

Some lads arrived in the field later than others, with varying excuses about why. There were many others, more numerous as time went on, so that a senior officer would be asked, as we prepared to move up, "How many runners tonight, Sir?" They had, in any case, become a liability and any one of them could create panic within the ranks when under enemy presssure. There were also a select few who had enjoyed a quiet billet in one or other base depots, and were glad to volunteer for overseas service to avoid a spell in the glasshouse. Instead, they found their way out via a POW Camp.

Desert Warfare ws the most fruitless campaign of all. There was little doubt that the enemy commanders were more adaptable and made full use of their advantage and experience. Rommel, in particular, was a master strategist, repeatedly cutting off our columns which persisted in presenting a broad front, and which were always weak enough at certain places to permit a break through. This enabled easy circling, causing great losses in our armour, either by direct assault or by being left isolated and unable to re-arm.

There were also the incidents of bravery, such as the breakout of the Green Howards, when cut off at a spot near Mersa Matruh, named the "Baguish Box". They had waited for darkness and set off on the break-out singing "There'll always be an England" and they did it. Then there was the raid, by the Long Range Desert Group, on positions at Derna which, though successfully carried out, had overlooked the barriers posed by enemy air raid trenches. These trapped several trucks, forcing their passengers to find lifts on the remaining vehicles, before they pulled out.

All except for poor Davy Gunn, a lad from Wick, who had to find his own way back to Kufra Oasis. Despite the mileage involved, he safely reported at base on Christmas Day. He was first spotted at the door of his tent, casually enquiring "Is the rum ration up yet?" There were many such incidents, most of them unreported. These individuals were the cream of the country and, though I likewise volunteered for the Territorial Army and for every other duty during hostilities, my war was reasonably smooth. I considered it my good fortune, however, to have shared the company of many of these men, under all conditions. These lads, who survived the Desert, were later to be found wherever there was an enemy.Sadly too many of them failed to make it.

Part Four

Normal Service is Restored

Chapter Thirteen

My return to Kyle revived memories of my old friends, the Officers and members of the crews manning MacBrayne's ships, with whom I had shared duties prior to the outbreak of war. I was keen to see them all again. John Watson, for example, who had joined the Lochness soon after she had taken up service on the Stornoway run. Unknown to me, he had been recalled to the Royal Navy and had become Commander of a mine-sweeping flotilla which had become a by-word in home waters.Now he had returned to MacBrayne's to command the Clydesdale which was employed on a cargo service operating from Kyle to Stornoway, assisting the Lochness. We exchanged many of our war experiences and I was amazed to hear of his adventures while still in home waters.

He told of how he had returned from sea to a town on the south-east coast of England and had just moored alongside when an enemy plane appeared. His vessel narrowly escaped a direct hit by one of the dropped bombs, which exploded so near that he was blown overboard, suffering injuries which caused him to stay in hospital. His ship was the well known Green Pastures which, after he had taken over, had the words “Or Hell” added to the port of registration, Glasgow, on the stern. Many of his friends referred to him as “Slasher” Watson, due to his constant thirst for adventure. Although I don't know the details, I 'm told Captain Watson performed some outstanding acts, for which he was decorated. Though still a young man then, he told us that his first ship had been torpedoed in the Dardanelles during the Old War, at which time he was the tender age of fifteen. He was a remarkable character.

Quickly idleness beagan to pall and I was bored and visited Mr. MacDonald, Kyle Port Manager, informing him that I was ready to restart. He welcomed me with open arms and informed me that normal services were being resumed the floowing week. He suggested it would feel like old times for me to take up the early shift, as from Monday. I was taken aback and suggested that I would feel better if, for the first week, I was to take up duty on the 9.00am to 6.00pm shift, just to get used to the old routine again. He informed me, however, he just could not ask any of the temporary staff to take up duties at the unsociable hour of 4.30am, to deal with the arrival of the Stornoway Steamer.

To say I was surprised is an understatement but, before many weeks had passed, I was to learn that many changes had taken place during my absence. Conditions of employment now rested with the worker, rather than the employer, who soon discovered that, if he wanted any work done, he had to knuckle down to the terms agreeable to the Trade Unions. In this instance, I held to my guns and took up duty as promised at 9.00 am. When I then discovered that our worthy Chief Clerk, |John Budge, an old campaigner of the First War, had done the early shift, I felt forced to take up the early duty for the rest of the week.

As time went on I was to learn that, whule I was trying to do my bit in far-off places, many incidents were taking place in the factories, docks and other places involved in the war effort. These left much to be desired by those who were engaged in a life and death struggle abroad, in the belief that similar sacrifices were being made at home. The temporary staff were retained, despite the return of those from National Service. We were soon to realise that work which had once been covered by one clerk was now not even being covered by two. This state of affairs had also spread into Senior Management.

One of my first discoveries was the manner in which our salaries were paid direct to the bank, without any note of how the account was calculated. I took up the matter with the Port Manager who insisted I write personally to the Staff Manager which, of course, was highly irregular. I took the opportunity to dictate a letter to his secretary, who was on my side, and he, unwittingly, signed it with the other items for despatch. In due course, we were rewarded with a proper statement, covering all details, to every member of the Companay at the end of the month.

It was good to be back though, and each day brought back old friends who were returning ftrom far places, taking up where they had left off. Deep down we all had changed some and were more mature individuals who had had to look after ourselves under difficult conditions. We were prepared to work full time for a fair return but were just that bit different from the young lads who had waved goodbye several years earlier.
Services had now begun to get into the groove but we were all aware that the old pattern was broken and the experiences of war had created a new one. The last of the paddlers in the fleet, the old Pioneer was withdrawn from service in 1944. She had served Islay well for manay years and in her own way played her part in the historic era of the MacBrayne fleet.

The Locheil

The new Lochiel was now established on the West Loch Tarbert/Islay service, another production from Denny's – it was rumoured that when the

order for this ship was placed the stipulaton was " a shallow draught, broad beam and a good sea-boat. I think it would be agreed that she filled the bill. Under the command of Captain Lachie Beaton she brought a high standard of service to Islay and her carrying capacity for vehicles was soon to be felt on the Islay roads and holiday accommodation.
After 18 years first class service the old Lochness was replaced by the Lochseaforth. The new ship was larger than her prededessor and the disposal of the Lochness heralded the coming end of steam ships in the fleet. However, three other steamers were to join us, the following year when the MacCallum and Orr companay was acquired giving us the Dunara Castle, Hebrides and Challenger. These ships were as well known on the Western seaboard as any of the others and the "Dunara Castle" will always be synonymous with St.Kilda and the evacuation of 1937. This fine old ship went to the breaker's yard the same year (1948)

Now MacBrayne's were once again the sole operators to the Western Isles and maybe this was ominous. New ships joining the fleet were cargo vessels indicating that for passenger services the emphasis was towards improved bus links and shorter sea routes, to meet the needs of the ever increasing self propelled holiday traffic. The Glasgow/North Mainland passenger/cargo service was never resumed, thus this popular summer cruise became a memory and the exploits of the Claymore, Lochbroom and Lochgarry, a saga of by-gone ages. The Lochnevis continued on the Portree, Mallaig, Kyle service but already there was a suggestion for a ferry linking Raasay and Sconsor on Skye. Improved ferries linking Kyle and Kyleakin, and the likelihood of a bridge in the offing (offing has rarely turned out to be so distant !), pointed to the ultimate withdrawal of the Lochnevis. The improving roads across Skye, premitting the development of a shorter sea crossing to the Hebrides, had even wider implications. These then were signs of an inevitable future, with the certain disappearance of the ships and the unforgettable characters who manned them when my world was young.

When recalling these early pointers in later years, I wondered why I had ever returned to resume my duties with the company. but cherished memories of those crews and happy yesterdays seemed to leve me no choice at the time. My return to duty, as described earlier however, provided a big disappointment. The crowning let-down arrived on New Year's Day 1946. I was again on Early Duty – 4.00am to 6.30am, and 1.00pm to 6.00pm, if the ships were sailing to time. If not, whenever the job was done. On that occasion, when |I came on duty at 1.00pm, the rest of the staff were leaving for lunch - I thought. In fact they were leaving to celebrate. I ended my duty at 9.00pm with the prospect of reporting back on shift at 4.30am. It was some way to celebrate my first Ne'erday at home since 1938. I went straight to bed and, you can be sure, my last thoughts before sleep were “never again”.

No time was lost in making application for a change of scene and early the next spring I proceeded to Head Office in Glasgow, where I was to be based, having been appointed Relief Agency Manager. Needless to say, Kyle Agency was never included in my circuit, as the Management couldn't bear to think of my drawing Lodging Expences while living at home with my parents.

My introduction to Head Office was an eye opener- Out-Port staff knew little of how the “other half” lived. Glasgow staff knew as little of their conditions. To the lower echelons, salary scales were unknown, so comparisons were impossible. My agreement, of course, was that while in Glasgow I fended for myself and only when on Relief Duties at Out-ports was the Company liable for Lodging Allowances. I don't know what “Lodgings” conditions are like in Glasgow now, but I can assure the reader that in the mid1940s, they were somewhat scraggy - almost as bad as those experienced during the Emergency. I sampled a few places without much success and, for one reason or another, preferred to be out of the city. An evil rumour went round the ships' staffs at that time suggesting that I was a spy sent out by management to check up on Pursers and any other staff I thought worthy of mention. I was never made aware of this addition to my appointment but it took me some time to change staff opinion.

The summer season of 1946 was spent on the island of Islay, supplying relief at Port Ellen, Bruichladdich and Port Askaig in turn and, much to my surprise, renewing the acquaintance of several old friends who had seved with me during my period with the Argylls. I lodged with Donald Sinclair who was then running a thriving boarding house. He had been cook on the Tarbet to Islay service steamer for more years than he cared to remember and many an enjoyable evening was spent in his company, while sharing a "wee dram" His good lady cared for the guests while he fed them. The cuisine was of the best, with the highlight being Scotch Broth, so it was no wonder he was dubbed the "Scotch King." This was the first of several duty visits to Islay where I made many friends and of whom I have the fondest memories.

The early part of 1947 found me in Stornoway, on a special duty on behalf of the Ministry of Food, who were operating two charger ships - the Lothdale and the Rimsdale - between Lewis and Mallaig, in connection with the fish trade. My memory of this period was the wonderful six weeks of brilliant weather, when most of the rivers ran dry and Stornoway harbour was alive with salmon, trying to find their way into the River Creed. The late spring and early summer provided the best weather for many years and, as I had little to do because of the late start of the fishing season, I took full advantage, with daily dips in the sea.

As soon as the weather broke, and the fishing came to life, I had to begin to engage labour at the docks in Stornoway and realised that I had been living in a Fool's Paradise. I wouldn't have been surprised to discover that the large commercial docks like Glasgow and Liverpool had been sending their men up to Stornoway on courses to learn the ropes. During my first effort at raising a squad, I quickly discovered that they worked to their conditions. Despite their claims for time unworked, they wanted it both ways, and half shifts were not on. Quite obviously, they were already getting what they demanded but I was not inclined to give in. I found myself in some difficulty and, on discussing the problem with the ship's mate, asked him if he could provide a squad from the crew on the same rates. He readily agreed, but after lunch, when I visited him and found no work being done, he explained that he had had a visit from the dockers' representatives. He had been told that, if any of the goods were moved, they and the goods would be thrown into the harbour. Needless to say, we were at a impasse.

Those in the know, however, both in Stornoway and Glasgow, were busy trying to restore the status quo, by finding any excuse for my withdrawal from Stornoway. Within hours I received a call from my manager saying that the Islay staff were clamouring for holidays. Arrangements were being made for my relief in Stornoway and I was to proceed direct to Islay. This incident was an eye-opener to me on how labour conditions had changed during the war and were to become the nature of things to date.

For the next three years, I continued on port relief duties, either for holidays or illness cover, serving Mallaig, Portree, Tobermory, Lochboisdale and, of course, Islay, based between times at head office. Though footloose and free, it was inevitable that sooner or later I would settle down. I had been watching a lass from the South Side whenever she passed through my line of vision. This soon changed to a wee word in passing and a "Wink". Obviously this couldn't last and on the first day of May – Red Sunday, we walked out together for the first time. Unwittingly, she was wearing a red hat which was promptly removed and committed to a carrier bag. This was the beginning of many forays, culminating in an engagement holiday on the Isle of Man.

On 28th April 1950, Rena and I, in company with a number of our friends, went to church and later to the Marlborough Hotel, in Shawlands, Glasgow, near where Rena had grown up. In due course, I am glad to say, we were blessed with two children - Christopher William (Kit) and Beatrice Joan - who have been a great source of happiness to us both and helped to make up a very happy home.

One of the highlights of the immediate post war years was Mam and Dad's Golden Wedding Anniversary. Murdo had already gone to the great trouble and expense to make the trans-Atlantic trip home for the celebrations..... and they were only slightly dampened by his having turned up a year early. It was in that year that the Free Church of Scotland presented Dad with a special Bible, for his services to the church. For many years he had been the Precentor (leading the unaccompanied singing) at many West Coast and Gaelic services. In fact, his nephew, Duncan Fraser, from Inverness was also a Free Church Precentor, and it was often the case that when Communion was held in Plockton, Dad led the Gaelic service in the open air, while Duncan led the English one.

Before our marriage, Rena had been secretary to the General Manager and I had the distinct feeling that management would rather have us settled outwith Glasgow. The Port Manager at Kyle had just retired and Mr. Budge, who had succeeded him, had made a request that I become his assistant there. As an added incentive, management offered the Port Manager's house for our use. We gave the matter careful consideration and were almost persuaded to accept...until the Staff Manager, casually quoting the General Manager, said he'd been told to remind me that though I would live in the Port Manager's House that didn't mean that I would succeed to the managership when Mr. Budge retired. This, we thought, appeared to be a rather early decision for a vacancy which was not to occur in the immediate future. This resulted in a quick decision by us that if they were already that far ahead with their future plans, we had no wish to take Kyle under those conditions.

Chapter Fourteen

The Staff Manager was now in a quandry, like many of his kind in those post war years, and, I am afraid, this remains the bugbear behind the continuous failures in industry which still beset this land. He spent some days wailing about our refusal and bemoaning his difficulties with ungrateful staff. In sheer pique, he offered us Lochboisdale which was considered the most isolated and least attractive of all the ports. Much to his surprise we accepted. The present manager had denied holidays until I had come along the previous year. He was leaving the Company and I knew what awaited us there

In fact Rena and I enjoyed a very happy year, meeting a lot of nice people and enjoying long hours of sunshine, on beautiful sandy beaches which stretched for miles. With nobody in sight, we played golf on the Machar golf course, with red balls during the day, when the daisies were open, and white balls in the evenings. The steamers only called during the evenings, except for the odd cargo ship, which called once a week. Bridge parties were regular and, with no-one in a hurry to go to work in the morning, there were plenty of folk to be seen wending their way home with the rising sun.

Major MacKenzie, the worthy owner of Lochboisdale Hotel, who had retired from a police career in Canada, was the instigator of many parties and, in one instance, brought a bridge team from Aberdeen to engage a local team and play continued throughout the weekend. The island was a happy hunting ground for fishers, who had the choice of as many lochs as there were days in the year. Shooting was also popular and, in season, the choice was wide and variable. Many pleasant afternoons were spent in one of the many quiet corners of the island and the shores of Loch Skipport were particularly attractive as we spent our time lying in the sun and "whistling" to the seals.

On our arrival in Lochboisdale, we had been housed in the hotel until such time as other accommodation became available. It was hoped that some imported Swedish houses, being constructed at the time, might be made available for let when completed. Meantime we were able to find space in a croft house, which we shared with two holidaying families from Edinburgh, and much of our time was spent in their company, which proved great fun.

Soon afterwards, one of the newly constructed houses became available and, after a short sojourn in Glagow, we returned financially poor but with ample requisites to set up our first home. Much of the work was of a DIY type and standards were, to say the least, good and not so good. For example, we had purchased a sheet of corkoid to cover the kitchen flloor. With studious care, I drew up a plan with exact mearurements, showing every detail where cuts were required to allow a perfect fit. The job was completed perfectly, fitting exactly...upside down. However after a flustery few moments, we settled for a middle cut and final fit.

We soon settled to home life and quickly established our mode of entertainment - bridge nights, ceilidhs – and just getting on with bedside carpet knitting. Kenneth Drive occupied high ground overlooking the pier and the Loch's length out to the island. On a clear day, the outline of Rhum and Canna was visible in the far distance. We became members of the Church of Scotland, at Daliburgh, and made many friends. George Wilson, the owner of a local garage, spent much of his spare time in our company and was instrumental in introducing us to a lot of the more inaccessible corners of the island. Many memorable picnics were made possible by his kindness. Later in the year, when the gale season was with us, it was quite usual to open the back door of the house and sample the salt spume, which had been carried by the wind from the west side, some three or four miles away.

On one occasion, we were watching a ship trying to enter the Loch from the open sea and I called Rena to come and watch. Deciding to open the door to get a better view, the locked back door promptly burst open with a force strong enough to bend the lock-bar. A great struggle developed to jam the door before the roof lifted off. These were incidents of the wilder days and many stories survived of past years, such as the storm which had lifted Johnnie Clark's hen house, which was last seen in the air disappearing down the Loch. Most of the hen houses were old upturned boats and, no doubt, the disappearance of Johnnie Clark's could have been put down to the "call of the sea".

The evening arrivals of the ships always created a bit of excitement and on one memorable occasion I arrived at the pier when the Lochmor was already alongside. Sandy Mac, the Piermaster, advised that he had had a visit from a Minister, who had suddenly been called to the mainland, and he hoped that I could be good eough to find a berth on the Oban steamer when she arrived.

I went to examine the Manifests, already in the Store, and to be introduced to the enquiring Minister. To say he presented a strange sight is an understatement because he had the most remarkable nose I have ever seen. While he was talking to me, I couldn't look at him. his was true of everyone who saw him and anyone who suddenly met him face to face was struck dumb. I invited him to the office to get him out of sight. When inside, he discarded his nose and became Alex Macdonald, the Chief Steward of the Lochmor, who had been given this disguise to test his opposite number, the Chief Steward on the Lochearn. I was struck dumb and honestly had failed to recognise him. For the rest of the evening, I had a hilarious time watching him meeting people for the first time and laughing at how emabarrassed they were to be caught staring at him.

When the Lochearn arrived, I took him on board to introduce him to the Chief Steward. To watch his reaction was just out of ths world. He excused himself and asked me come inside his office, shut the door and with a shocked look exclaimed "What a hell of a nose!" This was one of the most unforgettable incidents of my life and I'm certain many of the onlookers who were on the pier that evening will also remember it and have another laugh.

Life on the island was generally peaceful and quiet and any exciting incidents were confined to the period between the arrivals and departures of the steamers on Mondays, Wednesdays and Fridays. If you happened to be in the right place at the right time you could listen to the latest griff concerning recent incidents or those of wartime vintage.

The adventures of the Customs Officer from the time of the wreck of the "Politician" were of particular interest. Then the "Staff of Life"was so carefully rationed and the older folks were in such poor circumstances when, suddenly, they were liberally provided for, and so close to their door. Some of them failed to outlast their supply. Those who witnessed the landing and securing of the goods, maintained that the secret caches of the time had never been properly mapped and remain for the diligent searcher.

At that time, some of the salvage occasionally found its way to the pier and anyone prepared to purchase could get a couple of bottles. There was little doubt that there was regular, but secret, trade, on the nights the steamers were at Lochboisdale. On one particular occasion, the Lochmor had been informed that a couple of bottles had changed hands and could be found on the Lochearn. Both skippers got together on arrival and quiet words were exchanged that two Customs Officers had travelled from the mainland on the Lochmor and were on the lookout for the trading of bottles. An unobtrusive sentry was posted on the Lochmor to watch any unusual activities on the Lochearn. Sure enough, during a quiet period, a sailor was seen to appear on the upper deck of the Lochearn with two bottles which were hooked to a "heaving line", eased over the rail, carefully lowered below the surface and secured there. After he had disappeared, the watcher from the Lochmor moved across, recovered the full bottles and replaced them with two empties. Neither crew ever made mention of the loss...and the gain.

While we were enjoying this lazy life, a rumour began that we were likely to be moved. One evening the Lochearn arrived from Oban and, when I visited the ship to collect the manifests, I was confronted by the Staff Manager and Auditor, who were on a duty tour. The Auditor, on learning that I would be supervising the discharge and loading of the ship, promptly requested my keys so that he could carry out a check of my books in in my absence. I was aware that this was a regular habit of his, but I am afraid this, in my eyes, showed a lack of trust. I was determined that this was one system that would not be condoned by me.

To say that I was upset is an understatement and, in handing over the keys, I vowed he was to learn, before this evening was out, that any future checks of my books, at whatever agency I was working, would only occur during my presence. As soon as my outdoor work had been completed, I returned to the office to find that he had completed the check and, very jocularly, informed me he had discovered a discrepancy in my cash of some £100. I was in no mood to share this fun. I suggested that, if there was a shortage in cash, both he and the Staff Manager had helped themselves and they could make a clean breast of things, otherwise I would have to resort to calling the police and have them searched. In future years I had many audits, but never again in my absence.

My term at Lochboisdale, however, was indeed nearing its end and Rena had broken the news recently that we were expecting a family. In these circumstances, perhaps a less isolated agency would be welcome. Very soon we were advised of my appointment to Inverness and, as there was no house available there, we arranged that Rena would return to her parents' home in Glasgow and, until such times as a house became available, I would require a return to lodgings. In due course, we moved into furished property in Inverness and our furniture languished in stores, of varying quality. It was our experience that our furniture fared very badly over far too many months in storage. Eventually the Company purchased a house and we settle in there.

The Company had been in the doldrums since the end of hostilities and was showing little initiative in trying to regain the ground lost during the war, particularly the summer tours and steamer cruises, which had been so popular up to 1939. Inverness Agency covered road transport services only but I was soon pressing for the return of the Caledonian Canal Cruises which had operated over so many years. The old Gondolier, however, was now a "block ship" in the Churchill Causeway, linking the Orkney Group of Islands. I was aware, though, that the Lochinvar was now withdrawn from the Sound of Mull service and would be an ideal craft for the canal. For some time, it looked very encourging and we reached the stage where the old piers were surveyed and reports submitted. Somewhere along the line, though, the spanner was thrown in the works and the ship ws sold to an operator, for cruising on the south east coast of England. The final act of the Lochinvar was particularly poignant. A year later, a private syndicate from Argyll, purchased the ship for cruising on Loch Ness. Sadly, the ship was wrecked on the north east coast of England while on her way north to Inverness.

Apathy was rife and rivalries within management boded ill for the future. In my little sphere, I pushed along, introducing new day and afternoon schedules and competing for private work. The result was a contented staff, with increasing rewards for the extra work involving driving and maintenance staffs. In turn I enjoyed my work and became involved in the various activities offered by the Highland capital (Chamber of Commerce, Sea Cadets and other local bodies). I also enjoyed my Saturday cricket, each week, which continued for six years. My family were growing up - Kit already in school and Beatrice yet to reach that stage. This was indeed too good to last and I was instructed to forward to Fort William at the earliest possible moment.

It was typical of the time, although such emergencies didn't occur every day, I had always suspected that, when anything went wrong, the immediate cry was, "Send Fraser", thus to avoid any inconvenience to Head Office Staff . As guests had just arrived on a weekend visit, I was

MacBrayne's Fort William Agency and AEC bus.

in no mood to meet this demand and only agreed to travel on Monday morning. This was another new beginning but this time would end with my departure from MacBraynes.

My arrival in Fort William signalled a very difficult time for me, and much worse for my family. They were forced to remain in Inverness for some six months before they were able to join me in Lochaber. Even then, it was again furnished accommodation until such time as the Company provided a house. All this time our furniture again lay rotting in damp storage in the old Corpach naval base.

Changes in management and clerical staff had taken place and I was able to make good the vacancies in the lower grades. The Company also invited applications for Manager, and the General Manager phoned one day to enquire why I hadn't replied to his circular seeking to fill the vacancy. Having had experience of the position for the past six months, I had no intention of making application, being perfectly happy to return to Inverness where, over the last six years, I had built up a happy relationship with the office staff, garage drivers and mechanics.

They included an outstanding Chief Mechanic, Angus Ross, who had served the company since 1912 in Inverness. He and I were the product of the village of Lairg in Sutherland and what more could one wish for. He was a remarkable person and his relations with the driving and mechanical staff made happy conditions all round. Unfortunately, the General Manager insisted on my making reply and giving him reasons for not being interested.

It was obvious to me, having experienced the daily situation, how much would be required to get the Fort William Agency back on its feet, with a worthwhile and contented staff. I was very surprised to receive a reply, from the Chairman of the Board of Directors, offering me the post of Northern Area Manager, including local control of Fort William. This to my mind, was a double-edged sword, as several applications for the vacancy at Fort William had been received. I'm certain that the members of the Board didn't see it that way.

Christie greets Her Majesty during her visit to Lochaber

Unfortunately, at this critical time, the General Manager had become ill and H.S.MacLauchlan was not destined to recover. Thus his assistant, one Charles Leith, took over and interviewed me at Fort William. I was persuaded to accept the appointment, with much foreboding, which unfortunately was soon borne out !

Much had to be done to re-organise staff and remind some of them of their duties, quite apart from ensuring they were carrying them out! In righting affairs in Fort William, I was forced to borrow clerical staff from other Agencies - Kyle, Mallaig, Oban and Glasgow - to keep things going. Needless to say, I wasn't very popular in some circles but, from my point of view, the uphill battle was "worth the candle."

I introduced a local Staff Welfare Scheme whereby a small deducation was made each week, to meet Staff Cafeteria expenses. The surplus, with interest, was used to supplement Sickness Benefit, paid by the National Health Service, to those off work with illness. Within a year, we were able to supplement the NHS contribution with an equal amount. The Fund grew fast and Head Office only discovered its existence after my departure, promptly ordering it closed down. I believe the balance was divided equally amongst the staff. Their Conditions of Service were vastly improved and Duty Rotas were introduced to ensure equal status for all. This was also condemned by Head Office but their attempt to cancel it out was thwarted by the staff, who threatened strike action. As far as I am aware, the rotas continued unchanged for some considerable time.

I had discovered that special duties such as Tours Hires were restricted to certain drivers, who reaped all the extra wages. Many of the driving staff had served in excess of five years and with the numbers involved, I introduced two rotas; rota number one to include all longer serving drivers and number two, the most recent arrivals who would move up whenever a vacancy occurred.

These changes proved popular and things began to look better. There were, however, some members of staff who were not helping the changes and the greatest hindrance was the regular visitation of the Transport Manager. A local man, he succeeded the previous Road Transport Officer and insisted on retaining his Private Office, adjoining the goods store, and on making use of the staff without my knowledge. The balloon went up, one Saturday, when I discovered all my goods staff on duty, without my being advised, loading up timber required for delivery to the new General Manager in Glasgow. That incident was the final straw and speeded up my departure from David MacBrayne Ltd after some 33 years.

Rena and I agreed there was little to offer in future service for us in MacBraynes. We decided to follow up the offers which had been made to us in Inverness some years before, by the then Head Postmaster. In little time he was in touch with prospects. In the summer of 1961, Rena and I, with Beatrice and Kit, began a new life centred on the Sub-Post Office in the sleepy railway junction of Aviemore. The quiet life was not to last long, but that, as they say, is another story.

****

The MacBrayne's Circle

Murdo MacPherson, at 67, is a retired Transport Manager who, in his day, ran a haulage fleet of more than twenty lorries. He now lives in Inverness but grew up in North Uist and, it was there, travelling by MacBrayne's bus to school each day, that his affection for the vehicles and their livery has its roots. The only buses on the island were MacBrayne's.

While still professionally conducting courses on commercial and passenger driving, he is a leading member of this group of enthusiasts who collectively own about a dozen roadworthy restored and preserved examples of these iconic buses.

1952 Bedford

Today the Circle has more than eighty members but, as Murdo remarks sadly, only two members remain from the staff of MacBrayne's buses.

While many members hail from or have connections to the West Highlands, perhaps more surprisingly a substantial number come from south of the Border.

Then there's the nature of the vehicles themselves. Murdo tells me they are really special as MacBrayne's always opted for the highest quality of bodywork, and specified the "mountain view" windows above the passenger seats, maximising the tourist experience. No other buses in the Highlands at that time, he says, included that feature. They were also maintained to the highest standard, a detail which aids preservation and restoration. He says members feel a great pride in preserving and working on these buses, and the ones maintained by him are not just roadworthy, they also pass annual MoT tests.

Murdo co-owns and has restored two buses but also maintains two others,

1961 Bedford

collectively owned by the Circle. Co-incidentally, some years ago, visiting my "almost" roots in Lochboisdale, I was shown over a beautifully restored MacBrayne's Bedford bus. It turns out to be one of Murdo's. It is also the same model as the bus in which I visited the drivers feet and pedals in the incident described in my Foreword.

The exterior is pristine with that iconic, red, cream and green, livery. Inside, it appears brand new, the pile of the seats is deep, as is the colour and the leather trim is perfect, showing no sign of wear. Above the seats, the netting luggage racks look unused. It struck me it must have looked exactly like that when it first went on service operating on Islay in the 1950s. His other interests are another Bedford from 1952 which entered service out of Portree in Skye. Then there are the more modern vehicles, with the engine alongside the driver, inside the bus. One entered service in Fort William in 1961, the other on Mull in 1967.

Many members of The MacBrayne's Circle are simply enthusiasts for veteran and vintage commercial vehicles but the quality of the MacBrayne's fleet, along with their unique West
Highland identity, means there are few vehicles as worthy of

1967 Bedford

saving. Murdo tells me members get great satisfaction from driving, or simply being passengers, in convoy to their regular meetings throughout the Highlands and Islands. He notes they turn heads wherever they go, with the reception reflecting enthusiasm and affection amongst locals and tourists alike.

Curiously,the graphic designer or coachwork artist who developed that memorable and eye catching livery remains unknown to his, or her, admirers in the Circle. The identity was apparently lost with the disappearance of the bus company itself into the Scottish Bus Group in the 70s.

****

About the Author.

Kit Fraser spent his childhood in a number of homes, and schools, across the Scottish Highlands: Inverness, Corpach, Fort William and, latterly, Aviemore. After graduating from the University of Stirling, D.C.Thomson, publishers of the Sunday Post and Dundee Courier, gave him his start in journalism. This proved to be a stepping stone to BBC Scotland where, in 1976, he joined the team establishing Radio Highland, in Inverness.

From there, his career progressed through radio and TV production to on-air reporting, before being appointed anchor of BBC Radio Scotland's news and current affairs programme, Newsdrive. Next came the nightly live Politics Tonight, set up to reflect and analyse the new devolved Parliament in Edinburgh. From there, promotion to Political Correspondent, serving both TV and radio, was a logical step.

It was from that position, after more than 30 years of dawn starts and midnight finishes, that he took the difficult decision to step down from the BBC, an institution he had admired from childhood, was proud to serve, and which he holds in high esteem to this day. Today, as a freelance writer and media analyst, he lives in Dunbar, East Lothian, with his wife Joanne.

****

27311004R00121

Printed in Poland
by Amazon Fulfillment
Poland Sp. z o.o., Wrocław